No RISK *No* REWARD:
Mergers *of* Membership Associations *and* Nonprofits

No RISK *No* REWARD:

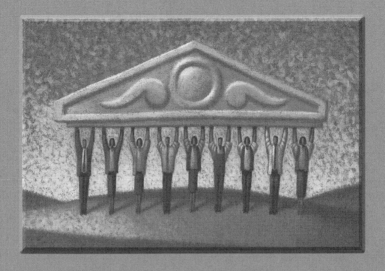

MERGERS *of* MEMBERSHIP ASSOCIATIONS *and* NONPROFITS

A handbook to help you prepare for the complexity of the process and avoid the inherent pitfalls.

Louise C. Dickmeyer, MNM

Andover, Minnesota

DISCLAIMER: This publication is designed to provide accurate and
authoritative information in regard to the subject matter covered. It is sold with
the understanding that the publisher and author are not engaged in rendering
legal advice, or any other professional service to the reader. If legal advice or
other expert assistance is required, the services of a competent professional
person should be sought. The reader should take note that laws and rules
applicable to their situation may change. It is the responsibility of the reader to
seek further professional guidance whenever necessary. The author, publisher,
and seller jointly and severally disclaim any warranty, express or implied, for
any general or particular purpose, including any warranty of merchantability.

ISBN 10: 1-931945-92-6
ISBN 13: 978-1-931945-92-9

Library of Congress Catalog Number: 2008941741

Printed in the United States of America

First Printing: February 2009

13 12 11 10 09   5 4 3 2 1

Expert Publishing, Inc.
14314 Thrush Street NW,
Andover, MN 55304-3330
Andover,   1-877-755-4966
Minnesota   *www.expertpublishinginc.com*

With sincere gratitude I dedicate this book to Billy, Tony, and Angie who all willingly yielded to me the many hours needed for its writing; to my mother, Dr. Aileen Eick, for her support on so many levels of its publication; and most especially to my husband, Bill, for his ever-constant support and urging to actually see this lifelong goal accomplished.

Table of CONTENTS

Appendices

FOREWORD

As I write this foreword today for my friend and author Louise Dickmeyer, I sit overlooking a majestic, if not slightly ominous, North Shore of Lake Superior near Tofte, Minnesota. November brings a brilliant low sun to the water—already churning and gray—in anticipation of another brutal, beautiful winter.

So, the blended aromas of hot coffee and chilled north woods air combine to bring a special clarity to my thoughts and recollections. My task, as requested by Louise, is to introduce her work on the mergers of nonprofits organizations. I am honored to do so, particularly since I fought at her side during some of the battles that produced important parts of this book. And, as evidenced by our writing, we both survived.

During the so-called battles, Louise served as president of the Minneapolis Chamber of Commerce and I as the board chair of the Bloomington Chamber of Commerce, two of the larger nonprofits of this type in the Upper Midwest. And, as timing so often is everything, our service coincided with a moment of tremendous upheaval in the chamber industry. Organizations like ours struggled to redefine themselves and find a new relevancy to attract new members and new capital. In a phrase, you grow or you die. We had both ceased to grow.

Back to my deck on Lake Superior: The power of the big lake is in its unpredictable nature. Sailors understand this very well—especially in November—when the water's surface can still look calm and inviting, only to turn in minutes into treacherous swells fully capable of taking down an ore ship.

So here were Louise and I, leading our respective organizations in what appeared to be rather calm seas. But underneath, enormous, systematic changes were taking place and a squall line was soon upon us. Thanks to strong, insightful leaders on our boards, we were able to stay ever so slightly ahead of this storm.

So here were Louise and I, stewards for the moment of two respected, venerable, prideful organizations whose foundations were silently eroding under our feet. Our members—our investors—our life blood—had all changed. No longer was the commitment of membership simply a community obligation that was beyond scrutiny. No longer were all of the largest membership investments made by local CEOs acting wholly independently. The sea had clearly changed.

What I can share with you from the shores of Lake Superior is that the charted course for merger is cluttered and imprecise. It is a divisive path where wrong turns by well-meaning folk are plentiful and damaging.

Still, today, I view the new organization that emerged from our combination and see much to be admired and feel only excitement and hope for the future. I attend original and vibrant events assembled by our new chamber and see new people and new companies participating in numbers we never achieved alone. Best yet, very few seem to recognize me—a fellow that had more than his share of publicity during the merger—and that is a great thing when you are trying to grow a volunteer organization. Therein lies the core of my last observation, that is, when success finally comes to the new organization and it is living and breathing of its own volition instead of relying on the echoes of the old, many of the original leaders will be gone—replaced by the next wave of enthusiastic leadership. Not forgotten, just replaced. That, too, can be a good thing.

I thank and commend my friend Louise Dickmeyer for recounting this adventure for a wider audience. There is wisdom embedded in the story and in the tactics applied along the way. The secret for those at sea in November is to bravely understand and appreciate those lessons of real value and scratch out those with none (there are lots of empty lessons) and do so with equal vigilance, intelligence, and passion.

—*John Jensvold*

PREFACE

This book is intended for use by membership associations and nonprofit organizations that are interested in merging operations with another organization. It presents the various aspects related to the merger process as well as the special considerations to be taken into account when merging membership associations.

The book also addresses the need for mergers in the nonprofit sector, why they should be considered as an option to strengthen an organization, the motivations that may lead to a merger, and the existing market forces that make that need more compelling.

The trend in nonprofit merger activity is on the rise and, relatively speaking, that trend is in its very early stages. As organizations approach a merger, they are better positioned for success by being prepared and aware of the complexity of the process and the inherent pitfalls.

Originally drafted as the capstone project for my Master of Nonprofit Management degree from Regis University in Denver, Colorado, this book explores a topic that had been of acute interest to me for some time. It seemed that the incidence of nonprofit mergers was on the rise and would become more commonplace in years to come. I was anxious to find out if that was indeed the case. I can assure you, it is!

In the course of the eighteen months from conception of my Masters project (book) idea to completion, ironically, my professional work life was consumed directly by a merger of two chambers of commerce—one of which I was president. It is this merger experience that is presented as the case study referenced throughout this book. My experience provided firsthand knowledge of benefits and drawbacks, pitfalls and success factors that can be present in any merger exercise.

I learned a great deal through the course of my project literature review and from my actual experience—which resulted, thankfully, in a successful merger. This research brought several facts into focus:

+ Many more organizations are pursuing some sort of restructuring than one might assume.

+ The trend in merger activity is on the rise. Throughout the book, organizations are cited that successfully merged. In addition, provided are resources that provide information on all types of strategic restructuring, from alliances to mergers.

+ In most cases cited, the motivation for merging or restructuring organizations is incredibly similar.

+ The drawbacks to all mergers are also similar.

+ Although the trend in nonprofit mergers is on the upswing, it is in its very early stages. This is borne out by these facts:

  • Relatively few published resource materials are available on the subject;

- There are relatively few experts on the topic—and yet I draw upon several individuals who have clearly earned that distinction.

+ Nonprofits and membership associations are relatively unaware of the need to consider strategically restructuring in any fashion. The argument is beginning to surface, though, and should be more prevalent over time.

+ Formal research is being conducted to study the integrations and alliances among nonprofits. One of the first such studies conducted is referenced in this book.

+ The individuals who have personal experience with a merger espouse a very similar process for accomplishing a merger. The consistency among them is fascinating.

+ There are many reliable resources to be drawn upon to successfully restructure a nonprofit—fellow nonprofit leaders, paid consultants, national organizations and foundations that advance the interests of the sector as a whole, and many articles and web sites to provide accurate and helpful information. Many are cited in this book.

This book will reveal to you many resources and should serve as a good how-to manual. In the process, this book will challenge readers who may or may not be committed to the benefits of merger or some aspect of restructuring. To this I remain firmly committed to the need to be open to explore mergers or at least some other such alliance.

Good luck as you contemplate the need for, and potentially pursue, a merger of your organization. Remember, it may be necessary to consider merger as a viable option for the health of the organization and success is entirely feasible. As you approach the intricate work to merge organizations, prepare as completely as possible—make use of any and all resources that may be available to you and then press on. The future of the nonprofit sector we care about may depend on it.

INTRODUCTION

"The melding of nonprofits into common interest organizations is a coming trend that will totally redefine the nonprofit landscape.
Those that are agile will survive and prosper.
Those that are not will lose mission components as they are swept away in this massive reorganization wave rather than learn to ride with the rising tide."

McCormick 2001

There are many approaches that two or more nonprofit organizations may consider to strengthen their collective pursuits. From a cooperatively run program to sharing of back-room services to a merger, many ways to restructure the organization's operations and efficiency exist. This book focuses on the most permanent and most challenging of those restructuring possibilities—merger.

Mergers in the nonprofit sector are becoming more commonplace. Nonprofit mergers can ostensibly appear to be relatively simple and uncomplicated. Unfortunately, this impression is false and can easily lead to failure. Without adequate preparation and understanding of the issues surrounding a merger, organizations may not be able to achieve their intended goal.

As noted by one veteran of the process at a meeting celebrating the successful merger of Family Service of Greater Saint Paul and East Communities Family Center, former President (retired) Ron Reed called the merger "a blending of two families and two distinct but compatible cultures" (Nonprofit World 1992). Interestingly, Ron Reed launched an initiative in 2007 within the organization MAP for Nonprofits, located in St. Paul, Minnesota, called Project ReDesign. The initiative is focused on helping nonprofits with assessment, project management, and implementation as they pursue mergers, program transfer, joint ventures, and the like. However, their primary focus is on assisting with mergers. In their first year of work, they had already served the total number of merged organizations they had hoped to serve over the course of the three-year pilot.

As two or more organizations consider a merger, a myriad of challenges will undoubtedly present themselves. Wading through these challenges, unprepared and unaware, will only make the challenges greater and will likely jeopardize the final outcome. It is well worth any staff's and board member's time and effort to apprise themselves of all information available from organizations that have worked through the process.

Theory and Practice Revealed

There are many approaches to what is being referred to in the sector as strategic restructuring. This may include an alliance of two organizations or a full-blown merger. The latter is the basis for this book. While many of the tenets are applicable in any type of restructuring, this information is geared toward accomplishing the ultimate goal of a full merger of at least two separate organizations.

This book is based partially on experience gained through the merger of two chambers of commerce. I have also cited and referenced countless examples of mergers that have successfully taken place in the United States and Canada. Those noted range from a combining of two United Way organizations, to national nonprofits, to foundations, to chambers of commerce. Cases noted include nonprofit 501(c) (3) organizations as well as 501(c) (6) organizations, including membership associations.

There are many examples of mergers available for study and comparison purposes to be found with nonprofit consulting agencies or in a search of the Internet and newspaper publications. Each merger, though, will take on its own life and constitute a varying array of issues to be addressed. While this book cites many different actual mergers that have occurred, it also cites cases where the merger failed and helps to reveal the reasons behind the failure.

Case Study

The case study I reference throughout the text is that of the merger between the Bloomington (Minnesota) Chamber of Commerce and the Greater Minneapolis (Minnesota) Chamber of Commerce. In this one example, I am able to present the many sides of the merger challenge. Using this case, I also address the unique challenges presented when members are involved in the decision to merge or not. This is a candid discussion of the political challenges and staff member challenges as organizations move through the process.

Valuable direction is offered to staffs and boards of nonprofit organizations about how to approach considering a merger, what to do during a merger process, and how to accomplish a successful merger. From experience, I can share that it is imperative, and most wise, to carefully study the subject and all of its complexity before approaching a merger. The better prepared staffs and boards are in pursuing a merger, the easier it will be for everyone involved. Adequate preparation will yield many good results and will prevent costly mistakes and may even eliminate some of the pitfalls. The breadth of topics to be considered is diverse, and I present those many aspects including: why consider merging, identifying potential need, and the partners with which you may wish to merge; differing organizational cultures and how to combine them; staffing—before, during, and following a merger; office location; implications with your membership; critical communications for a successful merger; financial, and legal considerations, due diligence, and merger agreements; structure of the new entity including governance and operations; and importantly, post-merger integration.

Membership Associations— Special Considerations

Endeavors to merge membership associations are open to additional political considerations due to their inherent make-up—the members. While bylaws are often written to vest the authority for such matters with the board of directors, not all organizations have this provision and, therefore, the bylaws of the organization call for a vote of the members to dissolve, or amend the legal structure of the organization. Member loyalty, member support and understanding of the need for a proposed merger, and ultimately, member vote are of critical importance.

In the case of the Minneapolis and Bloomington organizations, the bylaws did indeed call for a vote of the members. Even that process had several alternatives and various considerations. Ultimately, though, the most serious aspect was that the decision was left to hundreds of individual business representatives. It is one thing to have two well-informed boards of directors vote on the matter; it is quite another when there is a set of two or more diverse membership bases at varying degrees of appreciation and understanding of the matter at hand or the issues and solutions being presented. Selling a merger to the membership base creates a particularly difficult challenge.

Case Study

The Merger of the Bloomington Chamber of Commerce and the Greater Minneapolis Chamber of Commerce—November 2001

For the sake of explicitly presenting all aspects of a merger, I refer to the case study throughout this text. As an initial frame of reference, my involvement began with discussions for this merger in the first meeting of the staffs and executive committees, and continued through each aspect of the merger, right up through the actual tally of the vote. My responsibilities included initially "selling" the concept, responding to the problems and issues, and smoothing the bumps along the way.

My personal observations and comments will appear throughout this text as various aspects are presented. I hope that by presenting firsthand information on this case, the complex and issue-ridden process may be better understood by you.

Background

In the year 2001, the Chambers of Commerce of Bloomington and Minneapolis, Minnesota, represented the third-largest and the largest cities in the state. The Bloomington Chamber had been losing members and was unable to sustain its operations, staffing, programming, and communications, given its level of membership support. It was in a crisis mode. Leaders of the Bloomington Chamber approached their counterparts in Minneapolis and so began the merger discussions.

The organizations chose to take a soft approach to a merger and created what was referred to as an Alliance. The intent was to "date" for a period of nine months during which time the two organizations engaged in exploring the issues of a merger.

Organizational Histories

Bloomington Chamber of Commerce (BCC)—The community of Bloomington, Minnesota, had accomplished more than most other high growth areas in the United States in forty-five years leading up to 2001. Highlights of that period included the development of a burgeoning international airport—the world's ninth largest (in 2001);

and the Mall Of America—a world-destination retail and entertainment complex. In addition, two major inter-state highways run through Bloomington—Interstate 494 and Interstate 35. Throughout the region's growth, the Bloomington Chamber of Commerce had been at the forefront of providing leadership, resources, and programs in support of business success.

The Bloomington Chamber of Commerce boasted a membership basc in 1998 of nine hundred members. In the three next years, membership numbers dropped substantially, weakening the organization's financial base. The BCC recognized that it needed to strengthen the orga-nization in order to best serve its remaining membership and was, therefore, motivated to discuss a merger.

Greater Minneapolis Chamber of Commerce (GMCC)—The Greater Minneapolis Chamber of Commerce had been in existence since 1881. The GMCC members are located in the Twin Cities of Minneapolis and St. Paul and all suburbs in the region of which Bloomington is one. The majority of memberships in the GMCC were held by small businesses. However, the GMCC also had large corporate members such as Wells Fargo, USBancorp, Target Corporation, 3M, Cargill, Ameriprise (formerly American Express Financial), most of which still maintain their corporate headquarters in Minneapolis.

In the years leading up to the merger, the GMCC board had adopted an aggressive strategy to regain a community leadership position in public policy. Advocacy with a strong voice at the capitol was the central purpose for large businesses to belong to a chamber organization. In order to be truly successful in creating a strong position for advocacy, the GMCC board resolved it must continue to regionalize its efforts to assemble a broad membership base that consisted of thousands of members across the Twin Cities region.

In August of 2000, the GMCC Board approved a goal of "initiating formal discussions with local chambers specifically for the purpose of exploring areas where joint operations can either reduce cost or increase member value."

The Alliance

On December 20, 2000, the first meeting was held between the executive committees of the GMCC and BCC organizations. At their respective board meetings held the following month, an alliance was approved, which created a trial period in which to create the structure for the merged operations. This period was formally entitled the Alliance.

The Reality of the Situation

The good news was that the executive committees of each chamber were committed to a goal to strengthen their organizations for the long term and position their alliance as a meaningful business entity for the region. The boards had approved the alliance and understood the ultimate goal was an intended merger. The chief paid executives were anxious to begin work.

In hindsight, though, the staffs of both organizations were only remotely aware of the development, and most importantly, the ramifications of a successful merger. The two organizations were marching forward with a plan to completely integrate operations with a respectful assumption that, since they were both chambers of long standing, they were truly alike. In truth, the two were quite different. As work progressed, each one of these differences surfaced, and in some cases, caused problems large and small.

The Comparison

Aspect	Bloomington	Minneapolis
Mission –(abbreviated)	To improve the Bloomington business community.	To unite the region's business community in the development of a world-class competitive environment.
Size of Membership	600 members.	1,700 members.
History	45-year existence, suburban style.	125-year existence, metropolitan, big business style.
Decision Process	Volunteer-driven.	Staff-driven.
Technology	Relatively low-tech. Computerized, but operations not reliant on technology other than financial.	Technology investment had been substantial. New software to support membership operations, sales, communications. New web site.
Financial Management	No formal budget was written or approved over the course of several years. Part-time bookkeeper managed finances.	Formal budget written and approved by board prior to each operating year. Regular review of financial statements by executive committee and board.

Aspect	Bloomington	Minneapolis
Annual Budget	$325,000	$2.5 million
Staffs and Operational Structure	Interim/Temporary President. Two full-time professional staff in sales and communications. Three part-time staff in office management, programming, and finance.	President & Chief Executive Officer. Two Vice Presidents. Three Directors of Membership Services, Communications, and Office Management. Communication department. Formal public policy department. Formal programs and events department.

As you read, I offer direction in most aspects of this undertaking. Of those, there are a couple that (in hindsight) were the greatest areas of concern and required better handling. The first was determination of the succeeding chief paid executive. In the case of the Alliance, there were two individuals who were presidents of their respective chambers. The Bloomington position had been filled only one year prior on an interim basis. The Bloomington organization recognized it was challenged and brought a president in temporarily until permanent solutions could be implemented. In my opinion, having been one of the presidents, it would have been better had the matter as to who would succeed as the lone chief executive been resolved earlier in the process so as to avoid a fair amount of consternation and doubt, which surfaced, causing some jeopardy to the entire process.

The second aspect of concern was the acknowledgement, or lack thereof, of the costs of the merger. The staffs delved into the work of aligning and merging these organizations. No upfront consideration was given to the costs of the merger, either in hard cost or in the opportunity cost of staffs' time. (Both of these are addressed in chapter five.) To summarize, the costs mounted and both organizations' bottom lines went further and further in the red through that year and the next. Consequently, the challenges inherent to all mergers were exacerbated by financial worries. This aspect may have been either eliminated, or at least relieved, had adequate funding been secured up front, prior to the onset of the real merger work.

With the direction provided in this book and with direction gained from professional consultants, you should be able to navigate the issues efficiently and in good order.

The overall comment on what I learned from this case is prepare, prepare, prepare!

Epilogue: The merger became official on November 30, 2001. The vote was unanimous by the Minneapolis membership and was approved by a large margin by the Bloomington membership. As of this writing, the merged organization is operating well and has continued to refine how they present themselves in the market, further enhancing their position as an effective force for the business community they serve.

CHAPTER ONE

Why Consider a Merger: Organizational Motivations

"Oversupply is not a new problem in the nonprofit sector; it is the accelerating financial squeeze that brings new urgency to the oversupply problem."

Rick Smith, National Executive Director, Support Centers of America. La Piana 1998

The American Landscape

During an economic period in America where mergers within the for-profit community are prevalent, it is worthwhile to explore the benefits derived by nonprofit organizations merging their operations. For-profit mergers are intended to reduce the costs of operations, increase profits, and expand market share. Nonprofits may gain some of those same benefits, and more, by consolidating operations and reducing redundancy between organizations.

A principle widely held among nonprofits who have merged is this—a merger should be mission driven as noted here:

A merger should be mission and service driven. It should not be about the agency itself surviving, but should be about the survival of services to clients. The services and missions of both organizations will have to be carefully examined to see if there is a connection that will make sense.

McLaughlin 1998

The potential for mergers exists between many organizations in a community. One only has to review a community's list of nonprofits and their respective missions to identify overlapping goals. When those overlaps occur, a merger might be considered by those organizations with similar focus and service territory.

How Did We Get Here?

There are several factors that demonstrate why it is time to seriously consider mergers in the sector among its nonprofits and membership associations. From a historical standpoint, America and its celebrated democracy distinguished itself from other nations in the world through its volunteer efforts. Nonprofits drove democracy in a new form. Alexander de Tocqueville recognized and celebrated this fact two centuries ago. Basically Tocqueville asserted:

The American penchant and ability to form voluntary associations for every purpose has had a dual impact. It has enabled the people to remain sovereign and it has also enabled them to establish comprehensive associations, mainly democratic. This sense of free association and a method of improving society, separate from the acts government have lead to the development of a flourishing independent sector.

Elazar 1999

Interestingly, what Tocqueville defined over two hundred years ago still stands today as a hallmark of our society.

The third bridge Tocqueville builds is between ideas, culture, institutions, and behavior. It is to be found in his contrast between [American] individualism and [French] egoism. In making that distinction, he emphasizes the way in which American individualism combines the spirit of religion with the spirit of liberty and leads to the establishment of free associations to provide a corrective to the kind of individualism that knows no bonds, which Tocqueville refers to as egoism.

Elazar 1999

Too Many Nonprofits?

While this American individualism set us on the path to developing the independent sector, have we reached a point where the sector is overbuilt? Serving a mission through the nonprofit structure was, and continues to be, a successful venture. As challenges have presented themselves in communities, well-intending committees and organizations have spawned additional nonprofits to serve those particular needs.

An unchecked proliferation of nonprofits has created a sector that is, in some quarters, simply overstocked. In a study released in June 2000, as a collaborative effort of Chapin Hall Center for Children and Strategic Solutions, the authors note, "Competition is a key factor in strategic restructuring. It appears certain industries or service areas are growing crowded with nonprofits and, in some cases, for profits and governmental organizations. Organizations are attempting to temper competition by cooperating or merging" (Gowdy, Kohm, La Piana 2000).

A Tally of the Sector

Back in 1989, it was estimated that the nonprofit sector was comprised of 1,140,000 organizations. Of those, 400,000 were member-serving and 740,000 were public-serving organizations. Member-serving organizations include social clubs, business associations, labor unions, political parties, and member cooperatives. The public-serving groups include funding intermediaries (30,000); churches (350,000); service providers (220,000); and political action agencies (140,000) (Salamon, 1992).

Since 1989, the sector has continued to grow at a rapid pace. It is estimated that each year in the United States approximately 30,000 nonprofits are created, further compounding the problems of increased demands for funding similar missions. That growth rate equates to an additional 360,000 nonprofits in the U.S. landscape since 1989 or, on average, 6,000 new nonprofits in each and every state. Can there truly be that many unique and distinctive missions to be served in our society?

Within the sector there is a growing trend toward mergers as the need to do so occurs frequently. This growing trend is seen, in part, due to the maturation of the sector that proliferated during the 1960s and 1970s. Tom Silk, a nonprofit attorney and veteran of hundreds of mergers and consolidations, believes

> *A number of thirty-something nonprofits have reached a point in their life cycle where their best work is behind them, while others have achieved a level of organizational sophistication that allows consideration of complex issues such as those raised by a strategic restructuring effort.*

La Piana 1998

Limited Sources of Funding

The funding for these organizations comes from a relatively small array of sources. Membership associations are, of course, funded by their members with additional support attributable to government at all levels plus income derived from special service contracts or products. Funding from public-serving organizations comes from corporate foundations, independent grantmaking foundations, community foundations, federated funders, and through professional fundraisers, including private contributions.

Funders in the private sector (companies) are beginning to scrutinize their many commitments to all organizations throughout the community in which they operate. While wanting to remain supportive, the breadth of that support, or how thinly they spread that support, is in question. The threat of a decreased level of support can be a powerful motivation for nonprofits to finally consider merging.

Finally, the landscape has changed in regards to the support of the sector by the federal government.

Federal devolution of responsibility to the state and local government (often accompanied by a decrease in allotted resources); increased competition from business, government, and other nonprofits; and two decades of taxpayer revolts have brought many nonprofits to a crisis point.

La Piana 1998

Other Factors—Skilled Leadership

The shrinking supply of skilled leaders is also a motivation. According to the Society for Nonprofit Organizations,

The demand for increasingly sophisticated management skills is on the rise, while low management salary levels are still the norm. Nonprofit leaders, many schooled in the idealism of the 1960s, are aging, and no clear vanguard has emerged with the requisite blend of human-service and management skills. The survival of many nonprofits is at risk. Only the strongest and richest in resources are likely to survive in the long haul. Combining forces with compatible organizations provides one positive scenario for addressing many of these issues.

Nonprofit World 1992

A Historically Prolific Segment— Chambers of Commerce

The chamber of commerce segment is one example in the sector that has proliferated beyond an arguable efficient level—particularly in larger metropolitan cities. These metropolitan communities are often made up of many individual municipalities, each of which established a business association to serve its pocket of commerce.

The numbers are surprising. In metropolitan cities throughout the U.S., there exists one larger regional chamber of commerce that competes with many other local chambers. In the early 2000s, examples provided by the American Chamber of Commerce Executives include:

City— Regional Chamber	Other Local Chambers in Service Area
Buffalo, NY	32
Chicago, IL	120
Columbus, OH	28
Dallas, TX	55
Houston, TX	45
Indianapolis, IN	31
Milwaukee, WI	37
Philadelphia, PA	45
Seattle, WA	39
St. Louis, MO	70
Washington DC	33

Not only are there individual chambers for each suburb and city within a metropolitan region, there are often convention and visitors bureaus and economic development groups, all vying for the same base of support—business, foundations, and governments.

Some staff leaders are particularly insightful on the matter. The need for combined, effective chambers of commerce reflects the same efficiency the for-profit sector is demonstrating through merging and streamlining its operations. According to Gordon Austin, executive vice president of the La Mesa (CA) Chamber of Commerce,

The creation of larger, regional chambers is the only way we're going to be effective in the future in providing businesses with services that they need and are willing to pay for. However, as much as we cling to the notion that every community—regardless of its size—should have its own chamber, the reality is that too many are underfinanced, without professional staffs and—for the most part—unable to provide the kinds of services that businesses want and need. With municipalities under ever-increasing financial pressures themselves, it is unlikely that many of them will be willing—even if it were desirable for them to do so—to subsidize local chambers to the extent that is needed in many instances, to make or keep them viable.

Austin 1997

Research shows that cooperative ventures or mergers tend to occur when organizations rely upon the same resources. In the case of chambers of commerce, this is exactly what has occurred. Large banking corporations, gas and electric utilities, and communications companies, for example, tend to belong to chambers of commerce out of self-interest and a concern for community. In areas where there are numerous chambers serving the central city and the surrounding suburbs, the member companies are obligated to do for one as they have for another. Therefore, they pay dues to a staggering number of like-organizations.

This over-capacity issue is now more readily acknowledged within the sector. The umbrella professional association, the American Chamber of Commerce Executives (ACCE), has for some time been studying and addressing the need to merge. At a retreat as early as June 1998, members of ACCE studied various facets related to effectively leading chambers in the market. Among other strategic directions, the organization began encouraging chamber executives to consider alternatives with several directives. One such directive addressed restructuring as follows:

> **Facilitate Mergers and Consolidations**—For many economic and programmatic reasons, more chambers in metropolitan areas will be merging. Chamber executives need to be aware of the potential pitfalls involved in mergers and how they can pursue joint or cooperative opportunities to reduce costs and increase effectiveness (Chamber Executive 1998).

The Sector's Response

Chamber organizations of all sizes throughout America have readily become more engaged in merger activity. Examples of mergers of chambers of commerce can be seen from the east to west coasts of the United States.

A growing argument is surfacing that clearly asserts that strength can be gained from joining forces. Such mergers are viewed as a means to strengthen the voice in business in a region and to improve intergovernmental relations.

As noted in the case of Lehigh County, Pennsylvania, the phrase "E Pluribus Unum" could be the motto of those who advocate chamber of commerce mergers. If the experience in Lehigh County is any indicator, the idea of drawing strength from unity appears to be holding true. The Lehigh County Chamber of Commerce, formerly the Allentown Lehigh County Chamber of Commerce, has seen two smaller business groups—the East Penn Chamber of Commerce and the Western Lehigh Business Association—come under its wing during 1999.

As a result of these alliances, the Lehigh chamber picked up about 135 new members and the smaller groups have gained access to the Lehigh chamber's wide array of services. Members of the smaller groups can now take advantage of Lehigh's administrative support, have greater networking opportunities with other businesses, and subscribe to Lehigh chamber's health insurance program.

Leming 1999

Members are increasingly seeing the sector for what it has become. There are simply too many organizations attempting to do the same thing. In the process, they are creating redundancy and inefficiencies, spreading support out thinly in the markets they strive to serve. By working together through formal mergers or other forms of collaboration, these organizations may complement each other and ultimately improve the return on investment by their constituents.

Other Mergers in the Independent Sector

United Way Organizations—As another example, up until 2001, two United Way organizations existed to serve the neighboring communities of St. Paul and Minneapolis. These were separate organizations with separate staffs, serving essentially the same mission and region. By 1998, many of their large corporate supporters doing business across the metro area were urging the executives of the two organizations to combine so that corporate sponsors could better support the United Way effort. The uniqueness of two separate organizations was getting in the way of the business corporations' ability to provide the support they wanted. The then-publisher of the Minneapolis *Star Tribune* newspaper put a stake in the ground by resolving that the prospect of writing multiple checks for essentially the same endeavor was finally unacceptable. He told both organizations in simple terms, "I'm writing one check. You figure out how to use it." The two organizations ultimately merged in February 2001.

The United Way example proves that even if a nonprofit organization or membership association does not reach the conclusion to seek a merger prior to the private sector forcing it, the result can still be very powerful. Their positive response to the challenge demonstrated a level of sophistication and savvy that should be copied. By demonstrating that nonprofit organizations "get it" and that they are aggressively seeking ways to eliminate overlap and the inherent wasting of resources, their private funders should support mergers enthusiastically, both in terms of funding and in their volunteer support.

National Foundations and Service Organizations—The incidence of national-level nonprofit mergers is prevalent as well. Even at this level, the motivation is similar to that of a community United Way or chamber of commerce, as in the case of Second Harvest.

Much like the for-profit world, executives at Second Harvest and Foodchain said they came together to create more efficiencies in their systems. With a merger price tag of $1.3 million, both organizations have the same goal: to get as much food as possible to hungry people across the country.

Gardner 2000

Another example of national foundations merging was the Rockefeller Brothers Fund, one of the nation's one hundred wealthiest foundations, which merged with the Charles E. Culpeper Foundation in 1999. The motivation for merging the organizations sounded a similar theme. The foundation officials felt that, by merging, they would create a more effective grant-making institution that would ultimately require few resources being directed to their administrative costs resulting in more money being available to support their mission and their constituents—the charities.

Other more recent examples include the merger of Young Audiences of San Jose and Silicon Valley and Young Audiences of the Bay Area in mid 2004. As announced in 2008, three community agencies that provide mental health and substance abuse treatment to patients on Maui will merge into one organization—The Aloha House, Maui Youth and Family Services, and Malama Family Recovery Center will combine to allow for more efficient and economical administration of programs. Another example, set in Charlotte, North Carolina, involves two of the area's oldest and best-known social agencies. Thompson Child and Family Focus and The Family Center merged to combine programs, services, and staffs, affecting services provided to thousands of abused and low-income children.

Determining The Need to Merge

A number of factors lead to the need to merge. The following checklist is a helpful reference when determining the need or level of interest in merging. Ask your organization these questions:

+ Does another organization in your delivery area provide the same or similar service?

+ If your mission closely resembles that of another organization in the area, is there obviously overlap or competition?

+ Is your donor base solid, or do you struggle to secure adequate funding for the short and long term? If you struggle, have you had to suspend delivery of service or been unable to expand capacity to serve your mission due to shortages in funding?

+ Have you been successful in recruiting qualified staff members, and the quantity and quality of board members and volunteers? Is there a vacancy in your chief executive position?

+ Is your mission still relevant to needs of the community and service territory?

+ Are your service users asking for something that you do not or cannot currently provide?

◆ Is an inadequate infrastructure or lack of expertise preventing your organization from growing?

The answers to these questions will ultimately drive you to consider if combining forces with another would strengthen your organization.

Cost Benefit or Lack Thereof

The benefits derived from merging vary from one scenario to another and so do the motivations. Based on the research for this book, the least of the tangible benefits to be derived is cost-savings; therefore, it should be the least of the motivations. Unfortunately, this is probably the most seemingly obvious potential benefit and the one that most leaders would like to expect. While some cost efficiencies are to be realized in the short run, it will take some time before they are realized in the long term.

This bears repeating; cost savings should be the *least* of the motivations for pursuing a merger. This fact has been borne out in any number of scenarios and is sanctioned by the Muttart Foundation of Calgary, Alberta, Canada. Leaders there concurred that while economic pressures were often a primary motivation for considering a merger, should this be the *only* motivation, the merger may fail. In addition, this organization's board and staff recognized the costs involved in the merger and learned that the potential financial efficiencies are not realized for at least one to two years or more following the merger. The long-term benefit in terms of costs may only be that the organization is able to contain the increase in costs more effectively.

Realistic Benefits

The perceived benefits associated with the combined membership in a chamber of commerce or other business organization has more to do with increased market share and the inherent positive ramifications such as:

+ Stronger, more unified voice in public policy initiatives;

+ Expanded audience for programs and events;

+ Broader array of programming options for members of all sizes; and

+ Larger network to support members' business growth.

In the case study experience, the benefits had little to do with cost cutting from an administrative perspective. Following the merger, there were still two office locations, the same compliment of staff members plus a few additions, and two sets of office equipment. Some savings were realized from integrated communications and a scaling back of communications tools and strategies. An additional area of efficiency was realized with consolidated financial management, but that was the extent of the savings.

Benefit-Enhanced Administrative Support

Other benefits may be derived from a merger when one organization, while still growing, does not have the staff support necessary and the burden on the volunteers becomes too unwieldy. This benefit was derived with the merger of the East Penn-Lehigh Chamber of Commerce. The president of the Western Lehigh Business Council revealed their organization had grown to a size where it was unmanageable by its top volunteer officers and welcomed the prospect of a professional staff taking over the day-to-day responsibilities.

Conclusion

As noted by researchers Gowdy, Kohm, and La Piana in their study "Strategic Restructuring. Findings from a Study of Integrations and Alliances Among Nonprofit Social Service and Cultural Organizations in the United States," the most common benefits were:

- ✦ An increase in collaboration on programs,
- ✦ Increased services,
- ✦ Improved administrative capacity and quality,
- ✦ An increase in market share.

Once you are convinced of the rationale of merging, careful study of an appropriate partner and motivations for pursuing this course are imperative. Given the proper motivation, the work ahead will make sense and be completely defensible as the process matures. But first you have to get started.

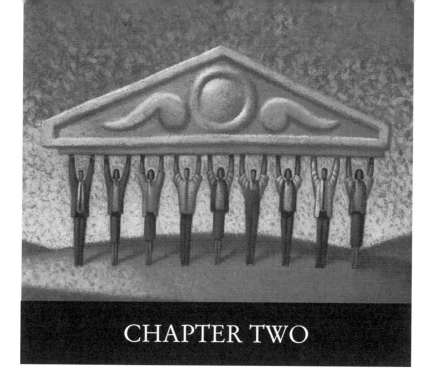

CHAPTER TWO

How to Approach a Merger and Organizational Culture

"Our environment isn't going to tolerate as many nonprofit organizations as we have right now. But consolidation is tougher in the nonprofit world because we aren't driven by bottom-line measurable results. Trust and progress take time."

Peter Goldberg, president and chief executive officer, Alliance for Children and Families, Milwaukee, Wisconsin. Gardner 2000

How To Start the Process

The volunteer leadership is perhaps the best group to initially approach the prospect of merging, although the paid executive staff members may also be effective. As the leader of an organization, the chair of the board, or the paid chief executive, once you have resolved the need exists to combine forces with a like-minded organization, potential partners must be identified with whom a merger makes sense and will strengthen the organization. In some cases, this is simple. Yet even though organizations may, on the surface, appear similar, the mission, organizational values, staffs, financial foundation, programming/work plan interests must be taken into careful consideration.

This is not to suggest that the mission, staffs, financial foundation, and work plan need to align perfectly. In fact, they can look quite different. The key is in envisioning combined operations. Do the two varying sets of interests and initiatives complement each other or compete with each other—essentially like oil and water? More importantly, an objective recognition of each of these components is required as you move through the merger process. Each has significant impact on how the organization operates.

One suggestion is to look for connections. Remember, the ultimate goal is to expand your capacity to serve your mission. Capacity relates to financial capacity, structure of your organization, program development, and constituency. You will be considering the connections between merging organizations due to the perceived fit to enhance, not detract, from building capacity to serve your mission. You will also look to some practical aspects such as your geographical location and reach. So give consideration to these various areas with an eye to expanding capacity:

+ **Financial Capacity:** What assets are present that, if combined, would strengthen your ability to serve?

+ **Constituents:** Are you serving similar constituents—is the service footprint identical or closely aligned?

+ **Organizational Structure:** This does not suggest that you have to find an organization that closely matches up to yours—but is there a basic structural premise such as functioning committees, governance structure—board of directors and officers? Is the organization in good standing in the region you serve?

The following are not designed to be a definitive yes or no filter to determine merger, but rather simply to suggest an array of considerations to keep in mind as you compare your organization to a merger partner candidate:

+ Do we share a similar mission?

+ Do we share a similar, or the same, constituency?

+ Do we have a similar operational style?

+ How do we compare in organizational style?

+ How do we compare geographically?

+ Do we each share a similar kind of public image? Is one of us better or less known?

+ Are we seen in a similar light within our industry or field? With equal professional perception?

✦ Do we each have facilities that are important to our mission?

✦ What assets can we bring, and what assets can we acquire, through merging with this organization, and vice versa?

✦ How will we increase capacity overnight (McCormick 2001)?

Approaching the potential merger partner is an obvious critical first step. La Piana offers this advice.

Approach a potential partner respectfully, in a manner that allows its leaders to save face and maintain their share of control of the situation. The merger process melds the mission, culture, and identity of both groups in the new entity. Fear of change, loss of autonomy, ego, habit, and culture cause nonprofits to avoid mergers.

La Piana 1994

Use of a Transition Team

The use of a transition team creates a core group to participate in the discussions and plans for the merger and to oversee the progress in general. Several key leaders should be identified from each board of directors of the merging organizations to assemble the team. This is also the group in which concerns should be addressed. They will be the best informed and best suited to head off problems as they arise. They are also the group to which the membership, as a whole, should look for information and direction. They are essentially agents for the process and should take their role on the transition team seriously.

The transition team for the Alliance featured in the case study consisted of thirteen individuals who were board members from each board plus the two presidents. The group was divided into three categories to address the following issues: 1) Finance; 2) Governance and Operations, 3) Communications, Marketing, and Expansion of New Entity. A timetable was established for each group to report back to each other en masse. (See appendices.)

Discovery Phase

In any merger, like any relationship, there is a preliminary phase of exploration and discovery. This refers to open discussion of expectations, pros and cons of the proposed action, exposing barriers or crisis points. It is essentially an exercise in full disclosure and one that is paramount to a successful outcome. All parties to the merger should make full disclosure at the beginning of the process. Legal representation may be involved in the conducting the due diligence investigation. All parties should share board minutes and other pertinent documents that illustrate their respective state of affairs. Financial disclosure includes review of past and future budgets and financial statements and audits, and disclosure of insurance policies and any outstanding claims. Each organization needs to understand the other's assets and liabilities to the fullest extent. Assets also go beyond monetary to include personnel, equipment, etc.

This phase goes well beyond the tangibles, though. It is the start of trust building and should be recognized at face value. One aspect of the case study merger was size;

one organization was larger than the other in membership, staff, budget, office location size, etc. The Minneapolis organization had been in place for nearly 125 years, the Bloomington organization for forty years. To some members, the size and tenure of the larger organization implied dominance. Not long into the alliance period were the words "take over" used to describe the intent of the formal Alliance. No matter how unfounded in fact that negative assumption was, those perceptions were real. It was that type of perception that needed to be dispelled through building trust.

I have always said that nonprofit management is both art and science. Never is that more true than when approaching a merger. There are practical considerations and people considerations, both carrying equal weight. Time hasn't changed much in this basic premise, as was directed in the article "Nonprofit Mergers: Perils and Possibilities" published in *Front & Centre*, Vol. 6, 1999, by the Canadian Centre for Philanthropy by two co-directors of a successfully merged organization, Big Sisters and Big Brothers of Calgary, Alberta, Canada.

Best practice dictates that in all aspects of a merger you encourage open and honest exchange. It is imperative that at the outset you both engage in full disclosure of all assets, liabilities, significant work, or challenges that occurred in the past but can still have an impact.

Practically speaking, look at your organizations with a focus on your respective missions and the values that drive the delivery of services today. Objectively review both organizations' strengths, then envision the best possible new organization. Also, take into account innovative work of other organizations that may be woven into the operation of the new.

A merger offers an opportunity to create a vision and establish ownership of its new direction. To be successful, exercise strong leadership from the board and staff. Make no room for waffling on the decision to pursue the vision of the merged organization. Once that vision is established, develop an integration plan to map the process of the merger to ensure that you address all of the necessary aspects. Assign teams duties in specific areas and create a blueprint for their work.

I strongly encourage the use of a trusted facilitator if you can afford to do so. A neutral party, and one that is knowledgeable about the process and pitfalls, can be invaluable and help streamline the process, keep everyone moving in the same direction, and arbitrate differences when necessary.

On the people side, get to know one another—staffs, boards, leadership. Trust is essential in a merger and it only comes with experience and exposure to one another on a face-to-face basis. You may wish to launch the work in a merger with small joint projects in order to build a base of trust. Keep all people informed with effective communication. This is a major contributing factor to a successful merger and one I address in chapter four. Deal with people's concerns and questions and create an environment for open exchange to validate their opinions. By doing so, you will create buy-in through the process and head off potential dissent more effectively.

Finally, through the hard work of the merger, try to move to the sunshine as quickly as possible. Don't get hung up on matters that can destroy better intentions. Mergers require thoughtful planning and implementation, but can get hung up on detail and negotiations and stall out or eventually stop entirely.

Utilize Reference Tools

Preparedness cannot be stressed enough. There are a number of good resources available in the market today that provide clear direction on how to proceed. While every aspect related to a specific merger cannot be covered, materials, including this book, will provide you with a good overview and prepare staffs and boards of directors for the ensuing work ahead.

Preparing the Staffs

The interest to merge will likely come from the paid executives or the board's leadership. Once the path is set and two organizations begin to consider all aspects of merging, the paid executives of both organizations should meet with their staffs to begin discussion on the merger. This preparation and enlightenment of the staff should take place as early as possible and often. It will take a number of discussions to ensure that all staff members understand the ramifications of the move—and to secure their buy-in.

The staffs of the prospective merging organizations will have to get to know each other and appreciate how they go about their business. It is an exercise in diplomacy and negotiation to coalesce staffs during this time. This becomes particularly challenging when the cultures in each organization differ.

Differing Cultures and How to Combine Them

Foremost, do not underestimate the importance of this topic. It can be a deal breaker of the first rank.

Culture manifests itself at many levels—in subtle and in obvious ways. As you simply walk into the office suite of your intended merger partner, it may be relatively easy to identify some differences in operations. As you review publications, or talk with staff members, you can also sense the differences in how each organization works. But, the ramifications and implications of cultural differences are harder to appreciate. Paramount to this entire discussion is the necessity to understand the power of culture and the potential for failure because of it. La Piana comments in his study of strategic restructuring on culture clash.

One result of a strong organizational culture is a slightly different subjective reality from that perceived by members of the next organization. In the normal course of business, this is usually not an issue, since visitors to an organization know they are visitors. However, during strategic restructuring, and specifically during merger negotiations, participants tend to forget this fact, by bringing their own organizational culture to the negotiating table, and to expect others to share their point of view. This subtle shift in expectations occurs precisely when each organization's most basic arrangements are being scrutinized, and its very culture is being implicitly called into question.

La Piana 1998

Also noted is that early identification and ongoing attention to culture nuances and other potential deal breakers is essential to a successful outcome.

Cultural differences are reflected in a variety of ways. They may include:

- ✦ **A staff-driven organization versus a volunteer-driven organization.**
  - Large, comprehensive staffs versus smaller, part-time staffs.
  - Technology systems and sophistication of information systems used by staffs.

- ✦ **Finances**
  - Sophistication of financial management. Does the organization prepare and guide their operations through the use of a budget?
  - Does the organization prepare and review regular financial statements?
  - Accounting principles may vary between organizations. Is the organization audited each year? Do they treat their income properly in the financial statements?

- ✦ **Communications**
  - Different strategies employed—how effective are they—are they old model functions—like a printed newsletter versus newer broadcast communications and electronic delivery?
  - How often are they communicating with their members?
  - Who is speaking on behalf of the organization?

- What level and type of publicity does the organization experience or seek?
- Is there a level of savvy in media relations?

✦ **Staff**

- Are there seasoned executives versus new staff members?
- What are the management styles of staff leaders?
- Are staff members experienced with specific skills or part-time generalists?

As two organizations begin to consider merging, they begin to work together and to consider how this will all look when it is finished. There are clearly opinions in each camp as to how well the other functions in each of these areas. Like any relationship, there will be a lot of "we" and "they."

With a common goal to bring together two operations with differing cultures, it is the role of the paid executives and the board's leadership to ensure the staffs and operations become sustainable. This inevitably means change and any change is difficult. Ultimately, some of the more serious cultural issues may be too difficult for staff members to overcome. You must be prepared for turnover of staff and executives.

Preparation is key to a successful merger. Some of the issues to be considered are obvious and relatively easy to understand the implications of each. Other influences, like cultural differences, are not as easy to read and anticipate. Take stock of these issues in a measured and deliberate fashion. Don't underestimate the potential pitfalls that can befall you in the process of combining two entities.

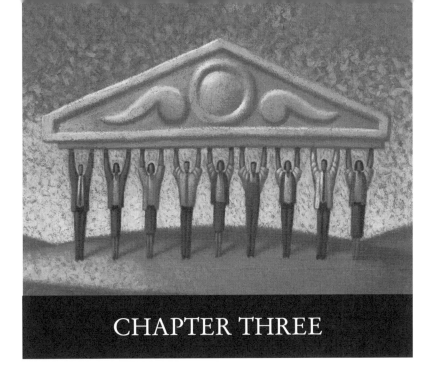

CHAPTER THREE

*Combining Staff,
Location, and the Members*

---

*"Blending two organizations who are set
in their ways is no small task. It involves more
than two individuals deciding to live together.
A successful merger is carefully planned, soberly
decided, and requires close and continuous
consultation with all who harbor reservations
toward the union."*

Ron Reed, former president, Family Service of
Greater St. Paul. Nonprofit World 1992

The Critical Impact of Staff

The consideration of staff in a merger is paramount. From the opening discussion on the possibility of a merger and throughout the entire process, the staff must be brought into the fold and made fully aware of the ramifications of the proposed merger and the process to complete it. Staff members have, obviously, various duties. Their perspective on why a merger is beneficial may be very different from the perspective of the organization's leadership. Plus, there are additional expectations of each department as work on the merger proceeds. Allowing staff members time to understand and get accustomed to what will be expected of them is an absolute necessity. They may have to change the way they do things, permanently, in order to serve the merged organization. This may require a good deal of work on the part of the paid executive. You do not want insurrection among the staff as you move closer to a merger.

In addition to the extra burden or work inherent in the merger process, there are personal and professional concerns about one's own future. These concerns will exist until the new job description is written and the organization is months into its new form. Each staff member, until that time, will have an array of apprehensions and questions.

Identification of the Chief Executive

Volunteer boards will do well to move quickly to resolve the chief executive issue first and allow that identified leader to lead the rest of the group. *Failure to move quickly to resolve this issue will only lead to struggle at various levels.*

Various scenarios might present themselves in any given merger:

+ Both existing executives may want the job of chief executive of the new organization.

+ Two executives may have varying interests, whereby one becomes the chief executive and one focuses on another area such as the operations, or finances, personnel, programs, etc.

+ Both may have no interest and, therefore, a search is imminent.

When a competitive situation occurs between existing chief executives, La Piana suggests this possible strategy:

+ When the committee meets for the first time, the members may ask the two executive directors if either one of them wants to lead the new entity. Both executive directors may want to be considered for the position.

+ At the same meeting, the committee would set up an interview process and notify the two executive directors of the materials they need to submit to the group for consideration and the timeline to do this. The committee might give the executive directors ten working days to submit their documentation for consideration.

+ Two weeks into the process, the committee's second meeting takes place and the two executive directors are invited to interview at different times. After the interviews, the committee reviews both candidates, discusses pros and cons, and votes for a candidate. Most often, committees will try to reach consensus on this decision because it may leverage more support at the board level.

✦ After the second meeting, the committee members go back to their boards to present their unanimous recommendation and the boards are asked to vote. Usually, a committee's unanimous recommendation should receive, at least, majority support from the boards. Less than unanimous support at this point may indicate problems with the way the committee was set up or with individuals or factions in the committee or board (La Piana 2001).

A merger committee in Bismark, North Dakota, anticipated a problem in the merger of two chambers of commerce and took aggressive steps. One of the merging chamber presidents had moved out of town, and yet no guarantee was presented to the other president. The chamber opted to open the presidency up to a nationwide search so that the new chamber could find a president who equally suited the needs of both communities. In this case, that remaining president did, indeed, eventually wind up with the job.

In other cases, the chief executive may take themselves out of the running at the very inception, planning a retirement at the time the merger becomes effective. Whatever the scenario, the transition team should address the issues firsthand and openly, disclosing their plans and intention to the paid executives and the staffs.

Restructuring the Existing Chief Executives

Other arrangements may be made to accommodate existing chief executives into the new structure based on their professional interests. The National Charities Information Bureau and Philanthropic Advisory Service of the Council of Better Business Bureaus merged into Council of Better Business Bureaus in 2000, and, in this case, the executive director of the foundation was chosen to head the new organization and the other merger partner executive was selected to head a major division.

In the case of the Twin Cities United Way, previously mentioned, the president of the Minneapolis United Way became the chief executive officer of the new organization. The St. Paul United Way executive was named the president and chief operating officer.

Securing Buy-In from the Staff

Great care and objectivity should be exercised when dealing with staff members. The chief executive should talk to each department and lay out the ramifications for their specific areas. Also, it is likely that additional work will be required of them over and above their regular duties. The demands of any nonprofit staff during normal times are usually great. Seldom do nonprofits enjoy an overabundance of staff, given fundings typical limitations. The demands on a staff during a merger period are overwhelming. Jim Colville, (retired) CEO of the Twin Cities United Way (Minneapolis) put it another way, "If you thought you were fully employed before, get ready to redefine that term."

It is not unusual that staff members at all levels will be threatened by a perceived *reduction* in staff. Experience dictates that this fear of job loss is usually exaggerated. Yet, while in practice, very few, if any, job losses are due to mergers; those fears and that of the changing culture and values are aspects to be regarded seriously.

Organizations that have experienced a merger widely hold the same opinion. It is suggested that announcing the tentative merger exploration to staff early in the process helps make the merger seem less threatening. This open approach also may create an aura of trust and under-standing that is essential to the success of the process.

It is likely that executive staff members are aware from the outset of the merger possibility. It is incumbent upon these leaders to take seriously their role in keeping staff in the loop, that is, informed and empowered to posi-tively influence the process. In not doing so, leaders may jeopardize the process.

Change creates needs. The people experiencing the vast amount of change inherent in a merger need the following:

1. Information—the more the better.

2. Support and encouragement. Staffs must be reassured that while the process will be chal-lenging, they will all wind up better in the long run.

3. A clear vision of where they are headed, and a sense of what the future will be like.

Also, permitting the staff to take part in the merger process through open reporting of progress and discussions about key decisions allows them to deal directly with their anxieties about the change rather than allowing anxiety to affect productivity and morale. If the staff is not adequately prepared to participate and support in all the work required for a successful merger, they are quite capable of stopping one.

Alliance Challenges (Case Study)

The pre-merger Alliance between Bloomington and Minneapolis chambers was established to allow time to integrate operations and to test the waters. While the intent of the alliance was to merge, the Alliance arrangement left much room for interpretation along the way as to the viability and wisdom of a long-term action like merger. At every level of the organization's operations there were areas requiring the utmost in service and efficiency by the Minneapolis staff to prove to our alliance partners that such a long-term arrangement was to their benefit. In other words, the actions and attitudes of each staff member were scrutinized. The leaders, in order to achieve the goal of merger, had to ensure that staff were on board and committed to the process.

Unfortunately, because the Alliance moved so quickly, those not closely involved in developing the agreement or not present at the press conference were left out of the loop, and staff executives did not take time, as they should have, to draw everyone together and bring them up to date to motivate them.

The staffs became frustrated due to their lack of understanding. When a few staff members from the BCC were relocated to the GMCC offices, the situation grew worse. Finally, the presidents pulled the staff together as a group. This provided an opportunity to explain exactly why it was a positive move and to explain the reasons why the GMCC could not remain status quo, but was actually strengthened by aligning with Bloomington.

Negotiating the Transition

The transition period begins really at the start of merger discussions. The transition period continues after the formal merger has occurred just in another form. The various aspects of post-merger transition are addressed fully in chapter seven. These following five tips offered by La Piana are applicable for the transition period as a whole—at the outset and following the merger—and will help you negotiate the transition with your employees:

✦ **First: Do No Harm**

As with doctors who take the Hippocratic oath, you must understand that the power to do harm is available to you. You could do harm by making decisions that would come as a complete shock to staff, taking managerial actions that appear thoughtless, or assuming that since staff will be resistant no matter what you do, you might as well just do something and move on. Think out the consequences of any decision and be prepared to deal with those consequences. The process is as important as the outcome.

✦ **Second: Be Aware of the Impact and not the Intention**

No one ever intends to have a decision go poorly, be misinterpreted, or blow up. Rarely is there malice on the part of management, but often there is a lack of appreciation of the impact a decision might have. Make no assumption regarding the historical goodwill you might have in the bank. Be prepared to deal with the free-floating anxiety that comes with organizational change. And keep in mind that in the light of organizational transition and an uncertain future, generosity could be seen as extravagance and efficiency as cold-hearted apathy. Have the patience to deal with negative reactions.

✦ **Third: Be Prepared**

Know that the process will be difficult, and that you have to be ready to respond to a changing environment. Preparing the leaders within the restructuring organizations to lead the transition must be a high priority. Part of this preparation is the acknowledgement of resistance and the development of tools and processes to address and engage that resistance.

✦ **Fourth: Keep your Focus Forward**

Keep the staff focused not on what they are leaving behind, but on what they are moving towards. There has to be a sense that the cost of the transition is worth it. You as the leader had better believe it, and it had better be true.

Keep yourself, your staff, and your organization as a whole focused on the mission, and on the future.

✦ **Fifth: Communicate, Communicate, and Communicate**

In the absence of information, information will be created for you. A crucial part of any employment transition is how it is communicated. It does not matter if no one will lose his or her job, that there will be more opportunities for career development, or even that benefits and compensation may improve, if no one knows that this is true. Creating a communication plan for the dissemination of facts is as important as the facts themselves (La Piana 2001).

The staff members were anxious to serve the Alliance and sought ways to integrate cultures and practices that have best served each of the operations. Tools that are useful to paint a realistic picture of the intended new organization include:

✦ Staff Rosters and Organizational Charts—which represent the responsibilities of both staffs and are meant to clarify that there is no redundancy in responsibilities.

✦ Job Descriptions—an overview of new integrated staff with explanation of new roles. These may ease concerns about loss of territory, influence, level of responsibility previously held. The descriptions also demonstrate the need for regionalization to strengthen both organizations and the community.

+ Staff Structure—Prior to, During the Process, and Following the Merger

The structure of the merged organization should be addressed as early in the process as possible. Sometimes it is not possible to identify what the roles of key staff may be if a significant shift is occurring with the overall surviving organization. But to the extent that the issues may be discussed openly, and all parties—every single staff person—is comfortable with his or her fate—then the process will go much further. Remember, staff members are key leaders, both good and bad, assenting and dissenting; they need to be on board, or the process will fail.

Location

Once a merger is completed, and long before the moment officially occurs, the issue of location will need to be resolved. Careful consideration of location issues must be weighed.

+ What location best will serve the needs of the members or constituents?

+ What are the costs of operating at a location?

+ Is more than one location needed?

+ What are the political ramifications of a specific location?

Beware; office location issues can lead to the failure of a merger. This was a contributing factor to the failure of a merger in Alabama. The Auburn chamber owned its building, but their intended merger partner, Opelika chamber, had been given office space by the city of Opelika. The members of the latter were not interested in having their chamber offices move to Auburn and that merger failed.

As two chambers of commerce in North Dakota pursued their merger, their leadership took some critical steps to address the location issue. According to the president of the Mandan-Bismark, North Dakota, chamber, both chambers owned their own buildings and to avoid a dispute over which building would house the new chamber, both chambers sold their buildings and built a new office.

Successfully Combining the Members

To state the obvious, in a membership association, the members are the lifeblood of the organization. They govern, provide the funding, communicate, and undertake the activities of the particular organization within their field of interest. They are the reason associations exist. So what special considerations arise as a merger occurs or is being considered in membership associations? The first concept is that of the values held by each set of members in general. Even though members may participate in the same industry, specialty, or cause, each may hold different values. The difference in values was cited as the cause for the ultimate failure of a merger of three organizations in 1999: The American Orthotic and Prosthetic Association (AOPA), the American Board for Certification in Orthotics and Prosthetics, and the American Academy for Orthotists and Prosthetics.

Trust becomes an issue among different membership bases and can also lead to failure. Robert Van Hook, CAE;

former executive director for AOPA; and now founder of Transition Management Consulting, Deale, Maryland, reported that members within the academy distrusted the trade association and questioned whether their needs would be served following a merger. That distrust was an obstacle to the merger. While the merger was viewed positively at the outset by staff and elected leadership in each of the three organizations, eventually the distrust issues were insurmountable (Bontempo 2001).

Case Study

In my experience, even though each set of members belonged to a chamber of commerce—(a business organization with a similar mission), their sense of the intent and value of that membership differed. Samples of those differences are as follows:

MEMBERS:	Bloomington	Minneapolis
Governance	Weak executive committee. Strong working board.	Strong executive committee. Policy board.
Volunteers	Volunteer-driven.	Limited volunteer opportunity. Staff-driven.
Programming	High regard for networking events. High volunteer participation in planning and carrying out events.	More limited participation in events. Public policy and government affairs programs were of strong interest.

MEMBERS:	Bloomington	Minneapolis
Access to Staff and Office	Members regularly met with staff members.	Interaction with staff limited to board meetings and board chair interaction with president.
Access to Other Members	High level of interaction at committee, board levels, and for social purposes.	Moderate interaction through events or committee.
Overall Perception	Community based organization.	Big business based organization.

Assuming a merger is completed, there are a number of things that can be done to meld the two groups. While some of the melding is driven by process, the underlying factor is differing cultures. In order to successfully blend the members, a culture for the new organization must be created. Two of the more obvious efforts might include:

✦ Rewrite the mission statement for the new organization.

✦ Set new priorities, goals, and objectives.

These transition matters are addressed in more detail in chapter seven.

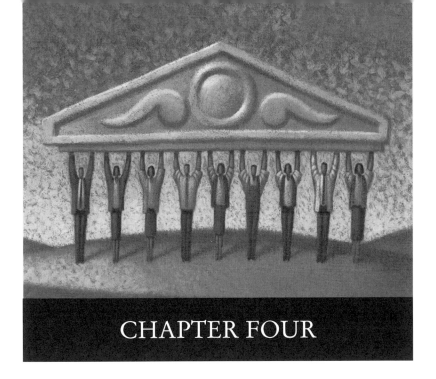

CHAPTER FOUR

Communications Functions

"The very essence of leadership is that you have to have a vision. It's got to be a vision you articulate clearly and forcefully on every occasion. You can't blow an uncertain trumpet."

Father Theodore Hesburgh, former president,
University of Notre Dame

How to Best Communicate Throughout the Process

Good communication is essential in the success of almost any venture in life. That need is accentuated in the merger process. Leaders need to stake their vision, articulate it clearly and with the utmost conviction. A mixed message or waffling of positions can crumble the foundation of the volunteers' willingness to consider a merger. Good and effective communication between each and all of the players will lead to a successful effort.

The communications function in a merger process takes on a multitude of forms. An ineffective communications strategy, or one that is not comprehensive, may do more to destruct the process rather than propel it toward the ultimate goal. Give a good deal of thought at the outset to drafting a communications plan, one that will serve internal and external audiences. Communication may be more of a public relations effort for the external audience, and more informational and directional for the internal constituents. How you communicate your merger process and how it rolls out will differ, too, with different sets of organizations in the mix.

A road map per se is presented here for navigating a merger process through its earliest stages through completion and the public announcements to herald a successful effort.

Note: The chapter uses the case study as a large part to discuss communications strategy. I use this specific example as a way to offer a clear understanding that may be gained through the study of an actual plan and the various aspects of communications. Pay careful attention to what is being communicated to whom at what juncture in the process to serve a specific purpose.

The Case Study

At the outset of the process, a formal communications plan was formulated by leaders of the organizations to present the prospect of merging the Greater Minneapolis and Bloomington Chambers of Commerce in the Minneapolis, Minnesota, area. The two organizations' boards of directors approved a formal Alliance in January 2001, which called for the integration of operations through September 2001. The ultimate goal, though, was to merge the Bloomington Chamber with the larger Greater Minneapolis Chamber. It was the task of the Greater Minneapolis Chamber of Commerce's staff to develop an organizational structure under the guise of the Alliance, which would prove to be acceptable to the Bloomington's membership and would, therefore, lead to a formal merger of the two organizations.

The role of the communications function throughout the Alliance period was key in persuading members that a merger best served their needs. We knew that the process needed to be underpinned by a communications plan that would articulate key messages related to our ultimate vision. That vision was essentially that all members would receive greater benefits of membership, and that the new merged membership would possess a stronger, unified voice in public policy matters. A successful communications plan would have fully informed and convinced the BCC members by the time the formal vote was to be taken.

The issue of a merger is highly sensitive. Board members and rank and file members are wary of a number of related consequences to such a merger. It is imperative in the communications strategy that all issues relating to staff, programs, finance, governance, and location are kept in mind as the communication function proceeded. These issues are complex and broad, infused with a lot of emotion and ownership. They may include:

✦ Protection of key staff positions and the individuals holding those positions.

✦ Continuation of program options currently enjoyed by the members.

✦ Identification of the organization within the community it represents.

✦ Relationships with local public officials and preserving the organization's position of influence in local public policy matters.

✦ Service to members as a whole.

Audiences

The complexity of the communications function may best be realized by reviewing the various audiences for which tailored methods and messages must be crafted. The audiences in the Case Study Alliance included:

Major Stakeholders/Funders—Those members totaled approximately thirty and fell in both organizations' membership base. Their role in the merger was important on several fronts. First, they collectively will pay the majority of the annual dues and provide the foundation of financial support for a functioning organization. In our case, it was critical that these members were positive about the Alliance and the proposed merger and were prepared to support it publicly. Consequently, they needed to ultimately choose to continue to support the merged organization and its mission or not. In addition, this group of members was also the likely target for fundraising to underwrite the mergers costs, the need for which is addressed in the next chapter.

Members—Of the 2,200 members that made up the Alliance, only about thirty were the largest of corporations. The remainder was small and medium-sized businesses in need of networking and programming opportunities in which to grow their business.

Dropped Members—Both organizations recognized that there were hundreds of members who had recently dropped their membership with both chambers. These dropped members were one of the primary target populations for attracting new members to further strengthen the position of the regional chamber.

Executive Committees—These two committees led the way in formulating the Alliance plan and advancing it to their boards. The executive committee had taken the risk of advancing the concept on behalf of the membership as a whole. It was imperative that each committee member was comfortable with the progress of integrating operations and was able to address the topic accurately and effectively whenever questioned.

Boards of Directors—While the executive committee advanced the idea of the Alliance, the boards put their stamp of approval on it on behalf of hundreds of members. They needed to be certain that those members' best interests were being served in the Alliance period and would continue to be served following the merger.

Staff Members—These staff members needed to serve the Alliance and eventually a merger organization. They were questioning the process but also seeking ways to integrate cultures and practices that had best served each of the operations.

Public Officials—Public bodies in the region had enjoyed a relationship with their chambers and had been relatively secure in the knowledge that they had local business support. By integrating two of the state's three largest cities into one business organization, public officials recognized that the rules of the game would shift. The staffs, while creating the regional chamber, had to ally the concerns of the public officials that their individual positions would not weaken with a change in the core leadership of the chamber.

Other Chambers—The Alliance was struck between only two of the forty local chambers in the Twin Cities region. It was the intent of the Minneapolis group to seek other partners as well, eventually bringing these local chambers into the regional chamber. A positive representation of the benefits was critical to attracting other chambers to consider joining forces.

The communications strategy needed to address the above noted audiences and to accomplish a singular, but complex, goal. That goal was to convince members in both organizations that a move to integrate operations would yield greater value for their membership investment.

Communication Styles

Several styles of human communication were employed to effectively promote the benefits and developments in the merger. These included:

+ Interpersonal communication between staff members of both organizations.

+ Small group communication, which took place between the boards of directors and executive committees of each organization.

+ Public and mass communication with the membership at large and with the general public.

+ Intercultural communication, which in this case, relates to the differing cultures between the organizations—one that is smaller and relies heavily on volunteers and small to medium business members, and one that is large, is mostly staff-driven, and has members from the smallest businesses to the corporate headquarters of Fortune 500 companies.

Supporters and Competitors in the Market

There were other key organizations in the region and state whose support was important to the regionalization of the chamber. Should they feel threatened in that process, they might attempt to block its development. In the Alliance, these included the Minnesota Chamber of Commerce, the Minneapolis Downtown Council, and the Minnesota

Business Partnership. There were also organizations that would likely fight the regionalization and not wish to see it succeed due to perceived greater competition.

Goals, Related Tools, and Key Messages

There were several goals for the plan, short and long term, and tools that were incorporated to reach the various audiences. Each communications function had a distinct purpose and none were independent of the other. The four specific functions that were covered in the communications plan included:

1. **Marketing**—This included marketing of member benefits as well as the Alliance concept.

2. **Public Relations**—Aimed at creating public awareness and acceptance of the regional chamber concept.

3. **Member Communication**—This is the perpetuation of communications that have taken place with members of both organizations over many years. Following the creation of the Alliance, an amended and enhanced communications strategy was needed to promote the Alliance, and to assure members that their services were not only being maintained, but, in many cases, were improved.

4. **Executive and Administrative**—This area included communications between the paid staff and the volunteer leadership;

communications with paid executives and the staff; and also staff-to-staff-meaning within each organization as well as between staff of both organizations.

The following table represents the type of communication, the tool used, an indication of the timing involved in the use of each tool, and key messages that were delivered in each case. The initiatives addressed in the communications plan ranged from the formal press conference used to announce the Alliance to the casual one-on-one communications that had been taking place in the development of the Alliance and merger plan.

Sample Communications Strategy

Element: Mass communication, Large Group, Small Group				
Tool to be used	Type	Audience	Timeline	Key Messages
Newsletter.	Written.	Large group—membership of 2,200+.	Bi-monthly.	Communication of new benefits communication of new dues structure. Consistent and sustained programming. Enhanced and expanded network. Strength in numbers for advocacy.

Element: Mass communication, Large Group, Small Group				
Tool to be used	Type	Audience	Timeline	Key Messages
Web site.	Written and interactive.	Over 655K hits a month from all over the world.	Daily hits and updates.	Integrated online Membership Directory. Programs offered with online registration.
Promotion of programs.	Written— broadcast fax.	Sent to over 1,500 member locations.	As needed. Weekly. Monthly.	Details on programs offered. Pricing, directions, registration details included.
Meetings with Members.	Verbal.	Paid executive staffs hold individual meetings with the largest members to discuss the plan for regionalization.	Upon request. May structure meetings with all large stakeholders.	Ability to strengthen the collective business voice on public policy matters on local, state, and federal levels.
Reports. Meeting Minutes.	Written. Verbal.	Committees. Public Policy. Ambassadors.	Monthly.	Specific committee activity may be integrated and will be more effective.

Element: Executive And Administrative, Office Operations, Small group				
Tool to be used	Type	Audience	Timeline	Key messages
Board Reports.	Verbal— Progress reports to executive committee, board, and committee members. Written— progress reports provided at meetings.	Executive Committee Members. Board. Staff.	Daily, weekly, and monthly.	Staff actions to blend activities in programming, and other initiatives.
Staff rosters.	Written.	Membership and Boards.	As needed.	Represent the responsibilities of both staffs' members and demonstrate no redundancy in responsibilities.
Job descriptions of new integrated staff.	Written descriptions. Verbal presentation tied to goals.	BCC & GMCC staff. Other potential partners.	Early in Alliance.	Explanation of new roles and integrated staff. Ease concerns of loss of territory, influence, level of responsibility previously held. Demonstrate the need for regionalization to strengthen both organizations and the community.
Operations.	Membership database.	Members. Staff.	Daily.	New system being implemented.

Element: Executive And Administrative, Office Operations, Small group				
Tool to be used	Type	Audience	Timeline	Key messages
Financial Management.	Monthly financial reports. Integrated budgets.	BCC & GMCC Boards and staffs.		Efficiency in operations and administration of combined organization.
Governance.	Written— Bylaws and structure of new organization.	Transition team.	Drafted and completed in 2nd & 3rd quarters.	Structure of new organization. Plan for integration provides for all sides interests to be provided for.

Public Relations Mass Communications				
Tool to be used	Type	Audience	Timeline	Key messages
Press Conference.	Written—script. Verbal —presentation.	Members. Public Officials. Competitors. Public.	January 24, 2001.	Positive move for both organizations.
Articles and editorials in local newspapers and magazines.	Written.	Public (including all of the above).	Ongoing.	Positive action for the community as a whole.
Press Release.	Written Verbal— Radio and TV Interviews.	Members. Public Officials. Competitors. Public.	Announcement of Merger on November 2001.	Success of the effort. Need to continue to merge nonprofits.

Components of a Successful Project

Success was measured by doing the following:

+ Successfully meshing staff members from the smaller organization into the larger.

+ Maintaining the membership base of 2,200. Approximately one hundred members belonged to both organizations. It was critical that those members not drop their membership due to a perceived lack of value in this merger, therefore doubling the loss of dues revenue.

+ Creating a governance structure that served the needs of two different populations and was a fair and equitable arrangement for the desired level of influence by organizational leaders.

As with any aspect of business, communication challenges presented themselves. In a merger process, these needed to be recognized and planned for in advance. As was stated in the opening chapters of the book, *prepare*. It is likely that the challenges you will face were previously encountered by the many organizations that have already accomplished a merger. Review of resources will prepare any organization to head off many of the challenges that are likely to surface.

Communications Plan and the Problem Areas

Timing
The time period in which the Alliance was proposed and approved was extremely short. This was a positive due to

the dire need of the BCC to find a solution to its financial situation.

The quick turnaround was probably facilitated as much by the readiness of the GMCC leadership, board, and staff to move toward the regionalization. The Alliance created a giant first step toward that goal.

While that organization's interest and ability to move quickly was positive, the quick and decisive action was viewed by one BCC board member, who was quoted in an early article on the alliance, as "secret maneuverings." That member felt as though the decision had been railroaded through without time for members to comment on the move. Even though that notion has since been dispelled, once something like that appears in the press, it is difficult to undo the negative perception. Be prepared to answer to the issue of the need for speed in your merger discussions.

The expediency of the Alliance had definitively scared the competition. For the Alliance and merger to be successful, the organizations needed to be ready to act in every facet and keep the process flowing. In the meantime, prior to the vote on the merger, the organizations needed to communicate positively as if it were a done deal.

Staff Issues

The staffs were totally confused by the speed and the intent of the Alliance. They became frustrated due to their lack of understanding. The appropriate message was eventually delivered and positively received by staff members. A better understanding was established and new rules are established to share information on the Alliance.

The Ultimate Goal of Regionalization

The GMCC Board had already approved a goal to create a regional organization. That was that organization's greater goal and it was intended that goal would be reached through a series of mergers with area organizations.

In the early stages of the Alliance, the GMCC staff needed to be careful to give attention through its communication practices to its only partner at that juncture, the Bloomington Chamber. The GMCC staff and Board carefully crafted messages that did not overshadow the Alliance by dwelling on the regionalization plan.

An Analysis of the Alliance Communications Plan

The analysis of the communications plan and the merger process lends itself to future mergers. With the merger now complete, several things were learned.

✦ As nonprofit leaders, we cannot communicate *too* much with our staff.

✦ The communication at the executive and board levels is of the utmost importance. In addition, one's conduct at these meetings is watched closely. GMCC leaders who attended the meetings were scrutinized and grilled by BCC board members as trust was beginning to build. A positive and honest response to their questions helped to create a prevailing positive aura. It was also vitally important that the smaller of the organizations did not feel as if it was being swallowed up or ignored by the larger.

The Minneapolis group had an established relationship with the media, which helped to pave the way for positive press on the developments. This is critical in the early stages of any merger process.

All communication has an effect. Whether it is a hallway discussion among staff or a formal discussion at a board meeting, the messages conveyed need to be positive. Should the Alliance have received lukewarm or negative reception from the board, members, public, partner organizations, or staff, it may have been doomed to fail before it had a chance to get underway. Absent the negativism, the staffs and board were then able to move ahead and build mutual trust.

The board members serving on the transition team need to quickly develop trust and take action on their appointed tasks. The staff needs to guide them with good information and in framing the myriad of aspects in a merger needing to be addressed.

The Alliance and subsequent merger of two chambers of commerce was a valuable project and one that serves as a model in other communities. In the final analysis, the success of that effort may be attributed as much to good communications as to the vision of the nonprofit leaders.

CHAPTER FIVE

Financial Matters

"It costs a lot of money to do this type of thing [restructuring and particularly mergers]."

Jan Masaoka, former executive director of the Support Center, executive director of CompassPoint.

Financial Resources

The financial matters needing consideration before, during, and after a merger cover a broad spectrum. Each facet must be addressed carefully and with due legal concern. Peter Goldberg, president and chief executive officer of the Alliance for Children and Families in Milwaukee and chairman of the Washington, D.C.-based Independent Sector noted, "You've got to have resources to make the merger work. Mergers create an important role for philanthropy. Where do you get the money to make this merger work? You've got to pay for all the additions, staff changes, board retreats, legal, accounting, etc." (Gardner 2000).

Prior to Merging

Areas to be considered before plans commence on a merger include:

+ Present disposition of finances of the merging organizations—while you are very familiar with your own financial status and position, you must gain a complete understanding of the financial status of the proposed merger partner and ferret out any areas of concerns or liabilities.

+ Financial Management—the system used to support the finances and the staff members assigned to that task. What was the level of sophistication of the financial management? Consider what it will take to integrate two systems.

✦ Assets and Liabilities—determine what they are and their impact on the balance sheet.

✦ The best financial management system to support the surviving organization.

✦ A projected budget for the merged organization should also be given consideration. I suggest that approximately three to six months before a merger becomes official, the staff should develop a one-year budget, and perhaps two to three additional years' budgets. These budgets will cover the aspects of merged operations, capital expenditures, and cash flow projections for the new organization. By preparing the full-year budget in advance, adequate time will be allowed for review, approval, and dissemination.

Managing Finances in an Interim Period

It is possible that back office operations are combined as a natural first step in a merger process. If you choose that course, further issues need to be weighed:

✦ Do you utilize separate accounting systems or integrate?

✦ Do you need to hire additional temporary staff to oversee the finances?

✦ How will you communicate on financial matters?

✦ How is information disseminated among staff, executives, and boards and committees?

Cost of the Merger

In addition to the standard procedural finance issues, the merging organizations must be aware of the cost of the merger. Board and staff leaders must carefully and realistically estimate the costs prior to undertaking any work on the merger.

The extraordinary and one-time costs associated with a merger are somewhat predictable and should be carefully weighed and considered. It is unrealistic to think that the merger will draw no further resources from the organization. Merger activity draws substantial resources—both in direct financial resources and in the opportunity costs as well as staff's time that is spent on merger issues versus business as usual.

The extraordinary hard costs may include:

✦ Consultant fees.

✦ Training.

✦ Legal fees associated with drafting bylaws and articles or incorporation and the filing of the latter.

✦ Systems integration—combining computer networks, financial software, connecting two locations to a central server.

✦ Personnel benefits plans.

✦ Corporate identity materials and all related collateral—letterhead, business cards, web site enhancements, signage.

✦ Finance systems and audits.

Cost Savings in a Merger

Often a central motivation for merging is to save costs associated with operations. While savings will be realized to some degree, they often are not realized in the early stages of a merger. As I've emphasized previously, the motivation should revolve around mission and strategy—not money.

There are some areas that may yield savings. These include:

+ Salaries—one chief executive instead of two, and other combined positions.

+ Administrative costs—managing one set of books versus two, office administration, etc.

+ Audits—one instead of two. (Although the first audit of the merged entity may cost more.)

+ Rent or lease costs—if offices are consolidated.

+ Insurance costs—directors and officers insurance and liability.

+ Equipment—reduction of equipment, again if offices are consolidated.

All financial matters related to the work to bring about the merger, or to operate post-merger, are important concerns. Attempt to amass adequate resources prior to pursuing a merger in order to effectively cover costs. The additional stress of pursuing a merger should not be exacerbated by financial worries. The leaders of the organization, by supporting the mission and strategy of the merger, should also be willing to support it financially.

La Piana offers a few tips in the overall financial scheme as they relate to one-time and recurring costs and savings:

+ Be prepared to call around and get estimates and quotes for various line items;

+ Many times you'll have to work with only the best estimates available;

+ It's OK to do guess work and not have hard figures; just be sure to let everyone know that is how this was done;

+ Whether accurate figures or best guesses, foot-note the source of your information;

+ List the costs and savings you identify in "one-time" and "recurring" columns for comparison purposes (La Piana 1999).

Approaching Funders

The intent to merge, as it is based on sound strategy to strengthen the organization's mission, is clearly a concept that the present funders and related funders would embrace. Therefore, it is this same group, those financially underwriting the organizations, that may be approached to assist in underwriting the costs of the merger. La Piana notes, "Funders may wish to sponsor broad educational and awareness-raising activities for the sector, and are then ready to assist those organizations that realize that a merger, consolidation, or joint venture might be an appropriate alternative for them to consider" (La Piana 1998).

Prepare the story and accumulate a list of transition costs and pitch your story. There are companies, foundations, and other organizations that will provide support.

In the case of the Alliance, funding was secured from several of the largest members who would benefit from the reduction of chamber organizations. They supported the merger and its intent to have fewer organizations in the market, thereby strengthening the lead business organization.

Dues Schedules

With the merged membership association, the board and/or transition team will need to determine what it will charge for membership. With any two membership organizations, it is unlikely that their dues schedule match up. In the case of chambers of commerce, especially associations that differ greatly in size, the dues schedule may be vastly different. The goal of merging is to create a better organization. Throughout the process, though, retention of members is key. Leaders do not wish to drive their support base away by pricing members out of the organization.

The dues issue was resolved in the Alliance when the BCC board adopted the GMCC dues schedule seven months before the merger was complete. For other organizations, it may not be so simple. Research and discussion with members and strong leadership from the volunteer board will help with the transition to a new dues schedule.

This aspect must be handled openly and fairly with input from both organizations in order to meld two schedules. This is, unfortunately, another area, that may lead to a failed merger attempt. Following the merger of five chambers in 1984 to create the Hampton Roads (VA) Area Chamber of Commerce, the revenue was significantly lower than was projected. Some of the original members of local chambers did not want a regional entity and dropped out, creating a greater loss of membership dues revenue than anyone had anticipated.

One tack used by a local chamber of commerce to ease members into the new entity was to give their members a break on their dues for a year. This successfully overcame this hurdle for a period while members got used to the merged organization.

The finances of an organization are a delicate matter. Unless the organization has substantial reserves, it must accumulate special funds, for the work of a merger is cumbersome and costly in a variety of ways. Preparing to cover the direct costs and projecting all issues related to financial performance during and after a merger is critical to a long-term successful venture.

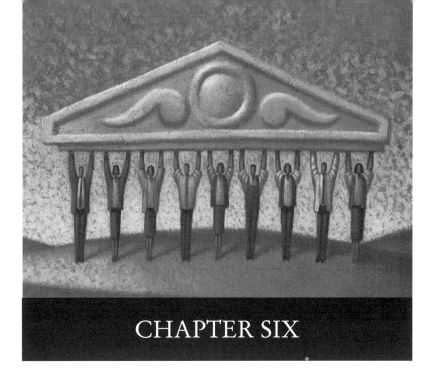

CHAPTER SIX

Structure, Governance, and Legal Considerations

"The final step: distribute copies of the signed merger agreement to committee members. Send a copy to your state's governmental oversight agency—then open a bottle of champagne."

Thomas A. McLaughlin, national nonprofit consultant, Boston, MA. McLaughlin 1996

Creating a New Organization

You are now well down the road to merging. You have made progress in combining programming, staff, and mission. You now need to create a set of documents to provide finality and proof of the action you are about to take and to govern and guide the newly created organization.

The surviving organization will need a name, bylaws, and articles of incorporation, and a board of directors. Reliance on your organization's legal counsel is a likely place to start. At the outset, though, consideration should be given to their level or expertise and interest in the project and whether they, or another more experienced counsel, should be used for this extraordinary work. General counsels of nonprofits may not have signed on for this type of specialized work. Ascertaining their willingness to serve in this capacity is quite important as the work commences. In addition, a discussion of fees should be undertaken. If counsel typically provides a certain amount of pro bono work to the organization, a clarification of what falls into that realm and what exceeds those limits is in the offing.

The Form of the Restructure

The structure is obviously the first area to be addressed in forming the merger or acquisition. This will have surfaced early in the discussions between organizations. As the legal preparations get underway, though, that direction must be identified so that the matter may be resolved appropriately.

One nonprofit expert offers this litany of ways a merger or acquisition option might be accomplished. Those options include:

✦ Purchase of Assets—One common approach is for one organization to acquire some or all of the assets (including programs and people) of another, with the intent of continuing the activities within the program of the acquiring organization.

✦ Acquisition of Stock—A few nonprofit organizations are formed on a stock basis so that control is vested in those who hold the stock of the corporation. An acquisition can be made by acquiring the stock of the entity from the present shareholders with or without payment, if state law allows such as transfer.

✦ Substitution of Members—A change in control can be accomplished by having the current member appoint representatives of the acquiring corporation as members of the acquired organization, and then having the old member resign.

✦ Substitution of Directors—In a non-membership corporation (controlled by a self-perpetuating board of directors), the existing board members (or at least a majority of them) arrange resignations and appointments so that all, or a majority, of the board is elected by the acquiring entity.

✦ Merger or Consolidation—Under some state nonprofit corporation laws there is a distinction between a merger, in which two or more entities merge but one of them continues as the "surviving" entity, and a consolidation, in which two or more entities come together and create a new consolidated entity. In each case, the continuing entity succeeds to all the rights, privileges, assets, obligations, and liabilities of the former organizations (Kramer 2001).

Due Diligence

Careful consideration must be given to what constitutes due diligence in the nonprofit sector. Clearly, due diligence must be undertaken for the benefit of all parities, but it may have differing significance in a nonprofit merger. Regardless of the form of the merger or acquisition, the acquiring organization should incorporate a thorough due diligence review of the organization being acquired. The acquired organization may be expected to make a series of representations and warranties, which should address financial issues, contingent liabilities, and pending or potential litigation. According to La Piana,

A substantial list of documents should be exchanged early in the negotiations process, for review by each party. The list should include documents relating to the organizations' legal structure and incorporation; IRS records; insurance coverages; personnel policies and structure; finance and fund raising; contracts, licenses, agreements and affiliations; capital and real estate; marketing materials; program activities; and any current or potential legal liabilities. The exchanged documents can then either be reviewed by each organization's attorneys and consultants, or, more economically, by the negotiations committee itself.

La Piana 2001

Drafting Bylaws and Articles and Related Approvals

Bylaws may be written using models from other organizations that exist in a form similar to that desired with the merger. In the case of the Alliance, the regional chamber of commerce was modeled after the Charlotte, North Carolina, chamber, adopting their bylaws with a few modifications to suit our particular case.

The Minneapolis Chamber organization's legal counsel (also serving as a board member) led this subcommittee to address the governance issue. Once the bylaws were drafted, they were carefully reviewed by all directors, amended, and revised until all parties were satisfied with the structure.

In the case of foundations, approvals must be sought on the merger and assurances provided that the donor's intentions would be carried out in the new entity.

In the Alliance, as the bylaws and the basic structure for the new entity were emerging, the organization reserved its intended new name with the Secretary of State's office with a nominal filing fee. This action secured the name of the entity, assuming the merger was approved.

Merger Agreements

Once the appropriate due diligence has been performed, the boards should proceed with drafting and approving a Plan of Merger and corresponding resolutions. Samples of these documents appear in the appendices. The plan of merger stipulates who will be the officers of the new corporation.

The following are possible items for inclusion in these unique merger agreements (McLaughlin 1996):

+ Assumption of debt
+ Assumption of liabilities
+ Board member nomination procedures
+ Board structure and composition (including committees and subcommittees)
+ Capital asset ownership provisions
+ Collective bargaining matters
+ Corporate form of new entity
+ Disposition of corporate entities
+ Disposition of major assets
+ Election of officers of new entity
+ Human resource issues (such as treatment of accrued vacation, sick time, etc.)
+ Initial market area or constituency to be served
+ Insurance requirements
+ Leadership appointments, as desired
+ Name of new entity
+ New board member terms

+ Policies for an employee separation
+ Salary and wage scales
+ Service continuation provisions, if any
+ Special provisions
+ Other agreements

Any other such operating agreements or addendums that one party or another deems necessary to provide adequate assurances should be written and approved as a part of this process. For instance, the Bloomington board drafted and presented an operating agreement, which provided for special considerations in the first year only of the merger. (See appendix H.) It addressed the treatment of program income, stipulated that an office would remain open as had been the case, noted the hours of operation of the Bloomington office, requested equal representation on the executive committee, etc. These items were of particular concern to the Bloomington board and staff. By incorporating the agreement into the plan of merger and approval process, the action was received more favorably by the Bloomington membership.

Calling for the Vote

If provided for in the bylaws, a vote will be taken if the structure of the organization, or its dissolution, may not occur without consent of the members. As was mentioned earlier, this opens an entirely different level of communication and preparation in order to achieve successful results. Members must be well informed on the matter on which they are to vote. Failure to inform will likely lead to failure at the polls.

The vote process may vary from state to state. In the case of the Alliance, each board was allowed to designate the method for the voting—via a membership meeting or by ballot. Bylaws will dictate the requirements for a quorum. The Minneapolis group selected a membership meeting to call the vote; the Bloomington group opted for ballot. (See appendices.)

Notice of the membership meetings need to be sent as prescribed by state statute. (See appendix K.) State law and the organization's bylaws dictate the exact representative eligible to cast the vote.

The Minneapolis meeting was held immediately following a board of directors meeting so that the directors were present and able to constitute a quorum, regardless of who else might have attended the membership meeting.

Ballots were sent to the Bloomington members that provided approximately four weeks for a response. A cut-off date for the voting process had been established by the board. All ballots were due in on the appointed date by 5:00 p.m. CST. The ballots were sent with a self-addressed, stamped envelope to allow for ease in the process. Note: The bulk of the ballots were returned in the first two to three days of the voting period.

Creating the New Board of Directors

The bylaws, of course, called for the governing board to be created. In the Alliance, there were two boards with individuals serving varying terms. It was decided early on that the boards would simply be combined and the bylaws would allow for up to one hundred directors.

Some organizations err by keeping both boards and combining them, though. This often creates an unwieldy board, according to Kathleen Enright, group director, marketing and communication, for the National Center for Nonprofit Boards, Washington, D.C. She suggests, "carefully considering the skills and abilities needed for the new board and selecting appropriate people. It's important that the board members understand that they represent the new organization and no longer place their loyalty with the old organization" (Bontempo 2001).

In the case of the Alliance, combining the boards was likely the only way to sell the merger. None of the existing board members were willing to step down and lose his or her authority. Therefore, it was decided to simply combine the boards, establish staggering terms among all directors, and essentially, allow the chips to fall where they may.

More careful consideration and internal discussion were undertaken to determine who the officers would be and who should serve on the executive committee. A nominating committee was formed, as had been the practice in Minneapolis. A chair-elect had already been seated both on the Minneapolis and Bloomington boards, but, ultimately, the chair from the Minneapolis board was selected as the new chamber's board chair. (She was, incidentally, serving on both boards and had, therefore, split her allegiance throughout the merger process.)

Beyond designating the chair of the new board, the chair-elect was carefully selected and members of the board were selected for the executive committee based on their vision and interest in advancing the new organization.

Combining Cultures

With the combining of the boards for governance purposes, comes combining of the boards' cultures. As I mentioned in chapter two, this is a challenging aspect of the merger as noted in this example of the merger between Second Harvest and Foodchain in 2000. The consultant who guided them through the merger indicated that it could take up to three years for the organization to fully integrate following a merger. Organizations are challenged to create a new culture among their board members. "You'll know you've created a merged organization when a board member sitting at a meeting can look across the table and see, not someone from the other organization, but someone from this organization" (Gardner 2001).

The notion of combining cultures may be better served if the organization broadened its board members beyond those previously seated in their respective pre-merger forms. This was found to be true in the October 1998 merger of the Support Center for Nonprofit Management in San Francisco and the Nonprofit Development Center in San Jose. In this case, their director, now in hindsight, advocates bringing in new blood for the merged organization's board. Executive Director Jan Masaoka commented on the following:

We decided to have eleven people from each of the former boards on the [merged organization's] board. One decision that the board made, in retrospect probably not a good decision, was not to recruit new board members for a year, so that the original twenty two would have a chance to get to know one another. The thought was to iron out some of the issues before recruiting new board members.

And, in addition, it was felt that twenty-two was too big a board. So people thought that in a year there would be some natural attrition and some people coming up on [the end of their] terms. Now I think we all realize it was a mistake, because it maintained a kind of "us and them" longer than there had to be. Once we had new board members, that started to evaporate much more quickly, because there were people who weren't "us" or "them."

La Piana 2001

Once the legal considerations have been addressed and the merger is officially complete, it is time to turn attention to implementing that original goal and motivation for the merger—remember—to better serve your mission, to increase program collaborations, increase services, increase administrative capacity and quality, and to expand your market share.

You now have the structure in place to accomplish these mighty goals. What's next?

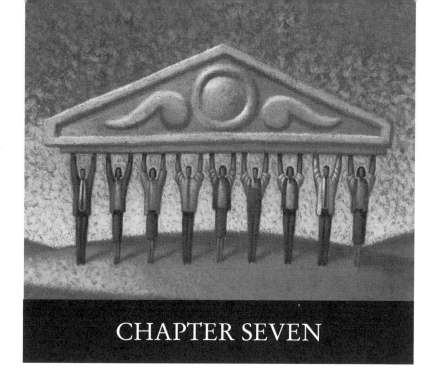

CHAPTER SEVEN

Post-Merger Integration

"I used to know my job pretty well. Now every day is something new."

Jim Colville, former CEO, (retired)
Twin Cities United Way, Minneapolis 2001

Celebrate

Even before the ink has dried on the merger documents, celebrate! Celebrate as boards, staffs, leaders, and a community. Celebrate and hail the good work of the organization and the people who brought to fruition a good and valuable effort. Celebrate, celebrate, celebrate! Everyone involved deserves it.

Public Relations Effort

Prepare in advance an official public relations campaign in order to announce the merger. In the case of the Alliance, we also had a crisis communication plan, in case the vote failed. But absent the vote by members, the organization should be able to gauge when the announcement may be made.

Control your message. The announcement of the merger is a rare opportunity to shed positive light on the organization and its mission. It is an opportunity to:

✦ Congratulate your present members on their new organization. (See appendix L.)

✦ Gain new members or supporters who like the mission and focus of the new organization.

✦ Attract the attention of other organizations that may also wish to combine forces with you.

✦ Provide recognition to the volunteers and staff who worked tirelessly to accomplish this goal.

✦ Encourage the sector in general to entertain mergers or other forms of restructuring.

✦ Recalling the information in chapter one, the trend for nonprofit mergers is on the rise. When one *successful* venture of this sort occurs, the more publicity the better. Remember, this type of activity is relatively unknown and is somewhat misunderstood. Within our respective communities, we should make every effort to publicize mergers to raise the public consciousness.

As your organization's merger efforts unfold, make no mistake, the work is being paid attention. Jim Colville, CEO (retired) of the newly merged Twin Cities United Way, addressed the boards of the Bloomington and Minneapolis Chambers about the United Way's merger effort. He commented that, "many organizations are watching what we are doing. If we screw this up, we set back cooperation in the region for a decade." So too, then, when you don't screw up and you manage to successfully complete the merger, make sure all of those watching are well aware of the triumph.

Building a New Organization—Integration

There may be a perception—or keen desire—that once the merger is finalized, the work will die down. In fact, this is the very time the real work begins. The work of integrating the organization completely, and creating the "us" environment at the staff and board levels is challenging and necessary.

Some suggestions for a successful integration process of nonprofits, or for-profits for that matter, are offered by Bliss and Associates and include:

1. Develop a crystal clear mission and purpose of the new organization. Develop three-month, six-month, and one-year goals of the new organization. These mission statements and goals should be so clear that it is virtually impossible for employees, management, and customers to misunderstand the purpose. Define the expected culture and operating style of the new organization. Gain senior management commitment as to how they will evaluate the success of the new organization.

2. Establish an integration team who is charged with developing plans, projects, and tasks to ensure the successful completion of the integration. This team should be given the financial and time resources to accomplish this critical step in the process. Depending on the size and complexity of the integration, this could be a full-time assignment to some or all members of the team.

3. Develop a communication process that will keep employees, management, and customers informed of the progress of the integration. Accept the notion that there is no such thing as over communication.

4. Identify obstacles to success. Gather the implementation team for a brainstorming session that will flush out all the possible obstacles and issues. Then, with each obstacle clearly identified, develop action plans that will prevent the obstacle from even developing in the first place.

5. Identify and define the processes of each of the merging units. Resolve to utilize the process that is truly the best without regard to where it comes from. Sometimes the best process actually comes from combining ideas from multiple sources.

6. Make it a standard operating procedure to evaluate each decision against the stated mission of the newly merged organization as a test of the correctness of the decision. Evaluate the decision-making process against the desired culture the new organization has decided to create.

7. Allow the staff to express their worries, fears, and anxieties about the merger. Also allow them to express their ideas, suggestions, and possible roles that they may be interested in assuming. People will be more committed and motivated to work harder if they feel as though they have been part of the solution.

8. Define the competencies needed of the management team in the merged organization and work to assess current management against those competencies as quickly and as objectively as possible. If there are to be any staff changes, decide and communicate those changes as quickly as possible, but not later than three weeks after the merger has been announced.

9. Identify some quick wins early in the integration process. Celebrate and publicize those

wins to everyone as a means of boosting morale and enhancing productivity.

10. Utilize positive communication styles such as providing honest feedback whenever possible, addressing rumors as soon as possible, and avoiding the secret meetings whenever possible (Bliss 2001).

Addressing The Culture Issue

As I mentioned in chapter two, culture is a huge consideration. It exists in every organization and continues as an issue to some degree between any two organizations following a merger. Two regional organizations in the New York City area cited the challenges as they strove to combine cultures. The obstacles included work styles, management techniques, and staff attitudes. When the Citizens Advice Bureau (CAB) and the Girls Club of New York merged, they retained the CAB name and remained in New York City. Yet, the board and staff of both groups had very different personalities. The CAB board, being community-based, made decisions through discussion and consensus while the Girls Club board had been more corporate using formal committees and drafting frequent reports. Following their merger, their director reported that while there had been a successful merger, there was resentment by Girls Club staff as CAB staff and programs moved into their building. Ultimately, several staff members left the merged organization. In the final analysis, though, the merger of the two boards resulted in a much stronger board.

Role of the Leader

Following the merger, the very important task for the paid executive, with the help of the volunteer leaders, is to make the cultures mesh.

The role of leadership, regardless of how you think of it, or define it, becomes the critical element of success in organizational transition. The captain's chair is looked to not only for direction ("Make it so"), but also for confidence and reassurance during uncertain times and new challenges. Lack of confidence in the leader leads to F & F—factions and friction. Groups will splinter and normative transitional issues will create extraordinary tension if a leader does not take up the specific role of transition manager successfully.

La Piana 2001

The president should first prepare the department heads by articulating the expectations and by being specific on how matters will be handled. Some edicts should be presented by the president effectively setting the tone for how the process fill flow. While recognizing that there will be challenges, the supreme goal is to make the merger work. There is no room for petty differences. For instance:

✦ The president should make it clear that anyone with a concern should come to them and discuss the issue. Maintain an open door policy.

✦ Staffs as a whole should meet together at each other's offices for monthly staff meetings.

✦ Staffs and departments, as they prepare for specific events, should meet together and with volunteer committees.

♦ Opportunities for downright fun should be
afforded, if possible.

Further insight on the role of a leader in the organization is offered by Jan Masaoka—formerly the executive
director of the Support Center and executive director of
CompassPoint of California. In October 1998, the Support
Center for Nonprofit Management in San Francisco
merged with the Nonprofit Development Center in San
Jose, which became CompassPoint Nonprofit Services.

*I think there were a lot of almost symbolic acts that
were important for me to do. To be physically present in
the San Jose office quite a bit. To have a lot of contact with
NDC [Nonprofit Development Center] board members.
To keep the San Francisco staff feeling like they weren't
being abandoned by our senior staff. To make a lot of calls
on nonprofits and funders and prospective partners myself
in San Jose. Those kinds of things. Demonstrating my
personal commitment to [making the merger work], to the
board and to the staff. Not just saying it but demonstrating
it was really a big deal. You need to get symbolic [and
demonstrate] an organizational and personal commitment.*

La Piana 2001

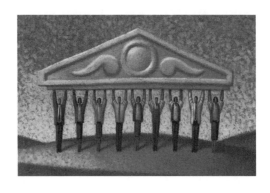

Transition Team as a Liaison Committee

The same use of a transition team or liaison committee is helpful in the post-merger era. A leadership group should continue to meet and resolve the bumps that are certain to occur along the way, especially in the first year following the merger. Parochial issues can be dealt with by the liaison committee, that may be made up of representatives from each respective community. By providing a fair and equitable voice on issues, the merger partners are likely to more readily become comfortable with the new structure.

While you can now appreciate the rigor involved in pulling off a successful merger of two or more organizations, it should also be apparent how important the post-merger integration is to actually realizing the full intent of this exercise. The merger itself is a formality, the real work begins the first day of the newly formed organization. While still serving your mission, heightened attention must be made to the care and feeding of staffs, members, boards, and the broader constituents at large. For a time, it will be nonprofit management on steroids, but eventually the merger process itself, all of its challenges and over-the-top demands will recede leaving in its wake a seamless operating entity.

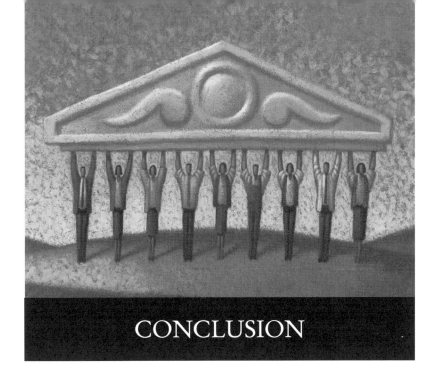

CONCLUSION

"A ship in port is safe,
but that's not what ships are built for."

Grace Hopper

A Successful Independent Sector

The effort to merge two organizations is, as my book has demonstrated, not an easy one. It is clearly an effort worth undertaking, though. As you do so, know that there are many resources—people, experts, publications, web sites, and supportive organizations you may turn to and upon whose experience and counsel you may rely.

The independent sector is undergoing transformation much like our for-profit counterparts. Our professional willingness to pursue and complete any kind of restructuring to improve and strengthen an organization's mission will demonstrate a new level of sophistication in the sector. Our market, those who fund us and those whom we serve, will regard the safekeeping of their investment in a new light. Given our independent recognition for the need to retool and reengineer the sector, and our action and resolve to see it done, imagine the efficiencies and the possibilities of our collective mission to serve society.

APPENDIX A

Transition Team Structure

[Alliance—Transition Team Assignments]

Finance—Four board members

+ Member dues schedule—levels for standard and associate memberships
+ Assumption of debt
+ Assumption of liabilities
+ Capital asset ownership provisions
+ Disposition of major assets
+ Insurance requirements
+ Transition costs

Governance/Operations—Four board members

+ Board structure and composition (including committees and subcommittees)
+ Board member nomination procedures
+ Election of officers of new entity
+ Leadership appointments
+ New board member terms

✦ Corporate form of new entity

✦ Associates

Communications, Marketing, and Expansion of New Entity—Four board members

✦ Initial market area or constituency to be served

✦ Expansion plan—additional markets to be served

✦ Related communications and marketing efforts

✦ Name of new entity

(Note: Presidents may serve on each of the individual subcommittees)

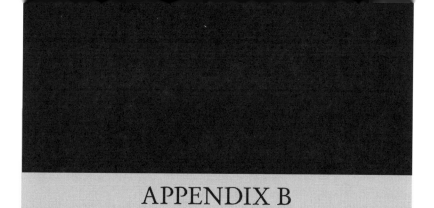

APPENDIX B

Transition Team Agendas and Duties

[Alliance—Transition Team]

Topics of Interest	Notes
Timing of Process	Merger, expansion, marketing
Structure of New Regional Organization	
Sample Organizations	U.S. cities with premier regional chambers
Dues Structure	
Governance	Board structure—advisory boards, etc.
Back Office Operations	Accounting, membership
Staffing	
Public Policy Initiatives	Committee form, structure, policies governing position statements—local, state, and national
PAC	Consider establishing and in what structure

Topics of Interest	Notes
Programming	
Financial Needs of Transition	
Expansion Plan for Regional Chamber of Commerce (CC)	Other areas to approach
Marketing & Communication of Regional CC	
Financial Needs	
Offices	Locations, equipment, etc.
Other?	

APPENDIX C

Timeline for Merger Process

[Alliance—Transition Team]

Timeline

✦ Preliminary review of Transition Team recommendations to take place at both organization's June 28 board meetings.

✦ Final review and approval sought at July 26 board meetings.

✦ Combined boards meet to discuss work plan for regional chamber at August 23 retreat.

✦ Invoices will be sent by July 31 to XYZ members with a renewal date of October 1. Payments will be due October 31.

✦ Merger vote meetings scheduled for first or second week of November. Notice sent mid-October. Both boards will collect proxies.

✦ Only members of the XYZ organization in good standing (dues paid by October 31) will vote.

✦ Date of formal merger to be determined—projected to be mid-November.

APPENDIX D

Transition Team Meeting Agenda

[Transition Team]

Agenda –

- ✦ Introductions—Staff and Board Members
- ✦ Background on the initiative
- ✦ Update on Alliance
- ✦ Issues for committee to address
- ✦ Timeline
- ✦ Election of Chair
- ✦ Schedule meetings

APPENDIX E

Sample Legal Documents

NOTE: Check with the state in which the merger will take place for all legal requirements. The sample documents provided in these appendices were applicable in the state of Minnesota at the time of the merger and should not be construed to be all encompassing.

Articles of Merger
PLAN OF MERGER
OF
ABC ORGANIZATION, INCORPORATED
AND
XYZ ORGANIZATION, INCORPORATED

Pursuant to the Minnesota Nonprofit Corporation Act, Chapter 317A of the Minnesota Statutes (the "Act"), ABC ORGANIZATION, INCORPORATED and XYZ ORGANIZATION, INCORPORATED, each a corporation organized and existing under the Act, adopt the following Plan of Merger (the "Plan") for the purpose of effecting a merger (the "Merger") in accordance with the provisions of the Act.

The names of the corporations participating in the Merger ("Constituent Corporations") are:

NAME

ABC Organization, Incorporated

XYZ Organization, Incorporated

Pursuant to the Merger, XYZ ORGANIZATION, INCORPORATED shall be merged with ABC ORGANIZATION, INCORPORATED. The name of the surviving corporation following the Merger shall be DEF ORGANIZATION, INCORPORATED.

The manner and basis of converting the memberships in the Constituent Corporations to memberships in the surviving corporation as a result of the Merger are as follows:

- ✦ On the Effective Date (as defined in Section 12 below), each membership in ABC ORGANIZATION, INCORPORATED and XYZ ORGANIZATION, INCORPORATED shall be converted into a membership in DEF ORGANIZATION, INCORPORATED the surviving corporation, on the same basis and terms applicable to each membership prior to the Merger.

- ✦ The Articles of Incorporation of DEF ORGANIZATION on the Effective Date shall be as set forth in Exhibit A and shall be the Articles of Incorporation of the surviving corporation.

✦ The Bylaws of DEF ORGANIZATION on the Effective Date shall be as set forth on Exhibit B and shall be the Bylaws of the surviving corporation.

✦ Each director of the Constituent Corporations on the Effective Date shall be a director of the surviving corporation to serve a remaining term equal to each director's term as a member of the board of directors of the respective constituent corporation immediately prior to the Merger or until their successors are duly elected or appointed. Following the Effective Date, the board of directors shall designate the members of the Organization Executive Committee for the surviving corporation. For the balance of [year] and calendar year [year], an equal number of representatives from each of the boards of directors of the Constituent Corporations immediately prior to the Effective Date shall be appointed to the Organization Executive Committee.

✦ On the Effective Date, the officers of the surviving corporation shall be as follows:

- Chairperson   name
- Chairperson Elect   name
- First Vice Chairperson   name
- Secretary/Treasurer   name

✦ Such officers shall serve until their successors are elected by the board of directors of the surviving corporation.

✦ Pending completion of the Merger, each
Constituent Corporation shall conduct its
operations prudently and in accordance with
its usual course and shall refrain from taking
any action, including incurring any debt or
entering into any contractual obligation, which
would have any material adverse effect on its
assets or business.

✦ Following approval of this Plan of Merger
by the boards of directors of the Constituent
Corporations, each Constituent Corporation
shall submit the Plan to a vote of the members
of such corporation holding voting rights to be
held on or before Month/Date/Year. The Plan
shall be adopted if approved by a majority of
members of a majority voting at each meeting
at which a quorum, if any quorum is required,
is present. If the Plan is not so approved by
the members of each Constituent Corporation
by Month/Date/Year, it shall be deemed to
be abandoned, unless the Board of Directors
of each Constituent Corporation approves an
extension of time for approval of the Plan.

✦ Following approval of the Merger by
the members of each of the Constituent
Corporations, officers and directors of each
Constituent Corporation shall promptly
prepare and file Articles of Merger with the
Secretary of State of Minnesota as required by
Section 317A.615 of the Minnesota Statutes
and take such other actions as they deem
necessary or appropriate to accomplish the
Merger.

◆ In connection with the Merger, the Constituent Corporations and the surviving corporation shall abide by the terms of the Operating Agreement attached as Exhibit C.

◆ Pursuant to § 317A.641 of the Minnesota Statutes, the Merger shall be effective upon the filing of Articles of Merger with the Secretary of State of Minnesota (the "Effective Date").

◆ Month/Date/Year.

ABC ORGANIZATION, INCORPORATED

By:_____*Chair Name*_____

Its:_____*Chairperson*_____

XYZ ORGANIZATION, INCORPORATED

By:_____*Chair Name*_____

Its:_____*Chairperson*_____

APPENDIX F

Sample Legal Documents

ARTICLES OF MERGER
OF
XYZ ORGANIZATION, INCORPORATED
INTO
ABC ORGANIZATION, INCORPORATED

These Articles of Merger relate to the merger of XYZ Organization, Incorporated, a Minnesota corporation, with and into ABC Organization, Incorporated, a Minnesota corporation, pursuant to Chapter 317A of the Minnesota statutes.

1. The Plan of Merger, dated as of Month/Date/Year (the "Plan of Merger") in fully executed form, is attached hereto as Exhibit A.

2. The Plan of Merger has been approved by each of the corporations participating in the merger pursuant to Chapter 317A of the Minnesota statutes.

3. Section 317A.811 is not applicable to the merger contemplated hereby.

Dated: Month/Date/Year.

ABC ORGANIZATION, INCORPORATED

By:_____

Its: Chairperson

XYZ ORGANIZATION, INCORPORATED

By:_____

Its: Chairperson

APPENDIX G

Sample Legal Documents

ARTICLES OF INCORPORATION

ARTICLE I
NAME

1.1 The name of the corporation shall be the DEF Organization (referred to herein as the "the Corporation").

ARTICLE II
REGISTERED OFFICE

2.1 The location and post office address of the registered office of the corporation shall be street, city, state, and zip code.

ARTICLE III
PURPOSE

3.1 The object and purpose of the Corporation shall be to [name mission and purpose]. The Corporation is organized pursuant to the provisions of the [your state] nonprofit corporations act, Chapter 317A of the [your state] Statutes.

ARTICLE IV
DISSOLUTION

4.1 Upon dissolution of the Corporation, all assets remaining after creditors are paid shall be distributed to one or more regularly organized and qualified charitable, educational, scientific, or philanthropic organizations to be selected by the Board of Directors, as defined in Section 501(c)(3) of the Internal Revenue Code of 1986, as amended.

ARTICLE V
DIRECTORS

5.1 Governance of the Corporation shall be vested in a Board of Directors (the "Board of Directors") whose members shall be nominated and elected in the manner described in the Bylaws. The Board of Directors shall have the power to create an Executive Committee and to delegate such functions, power, and authority to such committee as the Board of Directors may determine. The Board of Directors shall have the power to determine the number of directors and to adopt Bylaws that may contain any provision relating to the management of the business or the regulation of the affairs of the Corporation not inconsistent with applicable law or these Articles. The power to adopt, amend, or repeal the Bylaws shall be vested in the Board of Directors.

5.2 The Board of Directors shall have the exclusive power and authority to determine and approve all of the Corporation's policies and actions and to take any other action required or permitted of it by law or by these Articles. The Board of Directors shall take action by the affirmative vote of a majority of directors present at a duly held meeting except where these Articles, the Bylaws, or applicable law requires the affirmative vote of a larger proportion or number.

5.3 Any action required or permitted to be taken at a meeting of the Board of Directors may be taken by written action signed by a majority of such directors.

5.4 The affirmative vote of the majority of members of the Board of Directors present at a duly called meeting for such purpose shall be required to amend these Articles of Incorporation.

ARTICLE VI
MEMBERS

6.1 The Corporation shall not have authority to issue capital stock, but in lieu of shares of stock, the membership of the Corporation and the participation in the corporate rights and activities shall be based upon a system of dues to be established by the Board of Directors of the Corporation, and certificates of membership shall be issued, conditioned upon the payment of dues so provided, except that provision may be made in the Bylaws or other ordinances whereby honorary members are elected.

6.2 Members of the Corporation shall have no voting rights.

ARTICLE VII
POWER

7.1 The Corporation shall have the unlimited power to engage in and to do any act necessary or incidental to the carrying out of its purposes, together with the power to do or perform any acts consistent with or which may be implied from the powers expressly conferred upon nonprofit corporations by the Minnesota nonprofit corporations act, Minnesota Statutes, Chapter 317A.

ARTICLE VIII
PECUNIARY GAIN

8.1 The Corporation shall not afford pecuniary gain, incidentally or otherwise, to its members, directors, officers, employees, or agents. No part of the net earnings of the Corporation shall inure to the benefit of any member, director, or officer of the corporation (except that reasonable compensation may be paid for services rendered to or for the Corporation affecting one or more of its or their purposes).

ARTICLE IX
PERSONAL LIABILITY

9.1 There shall be no personal liability of the members, directors, officers, employees, or agents of the Corporation for corporate obligations.

APPENDIX H

Sample Operating Agreement

Exhibit C

OPERATING AGREEMENT
BETWEEN
XYZ ORGANIZATION, INCORPORATED
AND
ABC ORGANIZATION, INCORPORATED

This is an Operating Agreement between the XYZ Organization, Incorporated (hereinafter "XYZ") and the ABC Organization, Incorporated (hereinafter "ABC").

RECITALS

1. XYZ and ABC are considering merging the two entities to form the DEF Organization (hereinafter "DEF").

2. Articles of Incorporation and Bylaws for DEF were approved by the Board of Directors of ABC on Month/Date/Year, to be effective upon the earlier of any merger of ABC and XYZ, or Month/Date/Year. ABC approved a Plan of Merger for XYZ and ABC on Month/Date/Year.

3. The Board of Directors of XYZ approved the Articles of Incorporation and Bylaws of DEF on Month/Date/Year in connection with its approval of the Plan of Merger for XYZ and ABC.

4. It has been noted that a need exists for an operating agreement to cover matters outside the scope of the Articles and Bylaws of Regional and to indicate an understanding as to these matters between the parties.

AND NOW, THEREFORE, IT IS HEREBY AGREED:

+ Subject to Modification if Determined to be Appropriate by the Board of Directors of DEF:

+ XYZ Office. DEF will maintain an office in City, State, which may be in addition to other office locations, office hours to be Monday through Friday.

+ XYZ Programming and Events. To the extent that it is prudent, the current programming and events of XYZ shall be continued. Members shall be requested to pre-pay for events.

+ Staffing of XYZ Office. The XYZ Office shall be staffed at such level as determined to be appropriate by the Board of DEF. The staff of the XYZ Office shall report to the President of DEF or designee.

  • Duration of Operating Agreement. This Agreement shall remain effective through Month/Date/Year, unless earlier terminated by mutual agreement of the parties.

✦ <u>Formation of XYZ Area Council</u>. Upon completion of the merger between XYZ and ABC, a XYZ Area Council will be formed. NOTE: The establishment of areas councils was the governance structure preferred by the case study group. It is not required for a successful merger.

✦ <u>Operating Budget</u>. An Operating Budget for the XYZ shall be established by DEF for the period from the date the Merger is effective through Month/Date/Year, allocating a reasonable amount of resources for programming by the XYZ Area Council.

✦ <u>Event Revenue</u>. Net revenue from events sponsored by the XYZ Area Council shall be retained in a sub-account for the XYZ Area Council. The management of the sub-account shall be under the direction of the Area Council Board. In determining net revenue, DEF's overhead expenses attributable to supporting such events shall be considered.

✦ <u>Solicitation of Funds</u>. Funds may be solicited for events identified in the Operating Budget of the XYZ Area Council without approval of the Executive Committee of DEF.

✦ <u>Fiscal Year</u>. The XYZ Area Council will budget, plan, and operate on a fiscal year ending (date).

✦ <u>Composition of Area Council Board of Directors</u>. The current Directors of XYZ shall become the directors of the XYZ Area Council.

- ✦ <u>Membership Benefits</u>. Pending the completion of the merger between the two entities, new members joining, and current members renewing their memberships, shall all receive the benefits promised; i.e., member directory database, etc.

Dated: Month/Date/Year.

ABC ORGANIZATION, INCORPORATED

By:_____

Its: Chairperson

XYZ ORGANIZATION, INCORPORATED

By:_____

Its: Chairperson

APPENDIX I

Sample Merger Ballot

BALLOT

Proposed Merger of
XYZ Organization, Incorporated
and
ABC Organization, Incorporated

PLEASE RETURN COMPLETED BALLOT PRIOR TO
Month/Date/Year

This ballot is being furnished to all members of the XYZ Organization, Incorporated ("XYZ") for the purpose of voting on the proposed merger of that organization with the ABC Organization, Incorporated ("ABC") as described in the accompanying Plan of Merger ("Plan"). Pursuant to the Plan, if the merger is approved, the two organizations will be merged into one entity to be known as the DEF Organization. Memberships in each of the two existing organizations will be converted into memberships in the surviving organization on the same terms applicable to each membership prior to the merger. The Plan has been approved by the board of directors of each of the two organizations.

Please cast your vote on the merger by marking your choice in the appropriate box, signing the name of the person casting the vote, and returning this ballot in accordance with the instructions set forth below.

VOTE

On behalf of «Company»,

I _____ (_____),

    (Signature of person casting ballot)   (Please print name of person casting ballot)

❑ FOR the proposed merger

❑ AGAINST the proposed merger

Please return all completed ballots to:

    XYZ Organization, Incorporated
    Address
    P.O. Box
    City, State, Zip

[Specified number] completed ballots must be received from members of the XYZ Organization in order to satisfy that organization's quorum requirements for approval of the proposed merger. The ABC Organization, Incorporated has no quorum requirement.

The Plan will be approved if a majority of those returning ballots to each organization vote in favor of the Plan, so long as the XYZ's quorum requirement is satisfied. The Plan will be voted upon solely by use of written ballots. There will be no meetings to vote upon the Plan.

In order to be counted in the voting process, ballots must be returned to the appropriate address noted above by 5:00 p.m. month/date/year.

**PLEASE COMPLETE AND RETURN YOUR
BALLOT AS SOON AS POSSIBLE.**

APPENDIX J

Sample Merger Ballot

BALLOT

**Proposed Merger of
ABC Organization, Incorporated
and
XYZ Organization, Incorporated**

**PLEASE RETURN COMPLETED BALLOT PRIOR TO
Month/Date/Year**

This ballot is being furnished to all members of the ABC Organization, Incorporated ("ABC") for the purpose of voting on the proposed merger of that organization with the XYZ Organization, Incorporated ("XYZ") as described in the accompanying Plan of Merger ("Plan"). Pursuant to the Plan, if the merger is approved, the two organizations will be merged into one entity to be known as the DEF Organization. Memberships in each of the two existing organizations will be converted into memberships in the surviving organization on the same terms applicable to each membership prior to the merger. The Plan has been approved by the board of directors of each of the two organizations.

Please cast your vote on the merger by marking your choice in the appropriate box, signing the name of the person casting the vote, and returning this ballot in accordance with the instructions set forth below.

VOTE

On behalf of «Company»,

I _____ (_____),

(Signature of person casting ballot)   (Please print name of person casting ballot)

☐ FOR the proposed merger

☐ AGAINST the proposed merger

Please return all completed ballots to:

    ABC Organization, Incorporated
    Address
    P.O. Box
    City, State, Zip

[Specified number] completed ballots must be received from members of the XYZ Organization in order to satisfy that organization's quorum requirements for approval of the proposed merger. The ABC Organization has no quorum requirement.

The Plan will be approved if a majority of those returning ballots to each organization vote in favor of the Plan, so long as the XYZ's quorum requirement is satisfied. The Plan will be voted upon solely by use of written ballots. There will be no meetings to vote upon the Plan.

In order to be counted in the voting process, ballots must be returned to the appropriate address noted above by 5:00 p.m. month/date/year.

PLEASE COMPLETE AND RETURN YOUR BALLOT AS SOON AS POSSIBLE.

APPENDIX K

Sample Notice of Special Meeting

> **NOTE:** The Bylaws for these merging organizations required both a vote by the members, done with ballots, and approval by the board of directors. This special meeting was the final action in order to make the merger official.

ABC Organization, Incorporated
Address
City, State, Zip
Notice of Special Meeting of Members
to be held Month/Date/Year

To the Members of the ABC Organization, Incorporated ("ABC"):

The Board of Directors of the ABC has called a special meeting of the members of the ABC to be held in the [location], Address, City, State, Zip, at 8:45 a.m. Central Time, on Thursday, Month/Date/Year, for the purpose of voting on the proposed merger of the ABC with the XYZ Organization, Incorporated ("XYZ") as described in the accompanying Plan of Merger (the "Plan"). Pursuant to the Plan, if the merger is approved, the two organizations will be merged into one entity to be known as the DEF Organization. Memberships in each of the two existing organizations will be converted into memberships in the surviving organization on the same terms applicable to each membership prior to the merger. The Plan has been approved by the Board of Directors of each of the two organizations.

The Plan will be approved by the ABC if a majority of those ABC members present and voting at the meeting vote in favor of the Plan. Votes may only be cast by representatives of members attending the meeting, as the organizational documents of the ABC do not authorize voting by proxy. Each member of the ABC is entitled to cast one vote. The Plan is also being submitted to the members of the XYZ Organization, whose approval is being sought by written ballot.

The ABC Board of Directors has established Month/Date/Year as the record date for determining those ABC Members entitled to participate in the meeting and vote upon the Plan.

If a representative of your organization plans to attend the meeting, would you please advise <u>name</u>, title, by phone at xxx-xxx-xxxx, by fax at xxx-xxx-xxxx, or by email at <u>address</u>.

By order of the Board of Directors

_____
(Signature)

City, State
Month/Date/Year

_____
Name, President (of ABC Organization)

APPENDIX L

Letter Notifying Constituents of Merger

> **NOTE:** Organizations may choose how to communicate the merger to their constituents. This sample was derived from communication with the members of the merged chamber of commerce. In general, this type of communication tool is used to inform and more importantly to encourage continued support for the new organization.

Date, Year

Dear Organization Member:

Congratulations! Your company and its employees are now members of a new organization—the DEF Organization.

Members of the ABC Organization and XYZ Organization voted in favor of a merger this week, creating the [describe new organization's significance] .

As a member of this organization, your company will benefit from an expanded network of [X] member businesses, a stronger voice at the legislature, and expanded programming and regional resources. [Cite the strengths brought about by the combining of the two organizations.]

[Provide direction and assurance in how day-to-day operations will be handled. Make no assumptions that constituents know or understand these details yet.] We will retain offices in XYZ and ABC, and we will support three councils—the ABC Council, XYZ Area Council, and Small Business Council—that will deliver location and topic-specific member programs and volunteer opportunities.

[Make a bold statement articulating that vision and value add that you identified early on in the merger process. It is about to come true!] As a regional organization, we will successfully pursue an aggressive economic development agenda that is focused on recruitment of businesses and markets the city worldwide; advance a public policy agenda that addresses regional issues; and lead a focused effort to attract and retain talented, qualified workers and advocates for upgrading existing workers' skills.

This is the beginning of a powerful partnership and business initiative. Watch our web site for the latest news, and if you have questions about the DEF Organization, please contact me at xxx-xxx-xxxx.

Sincerely,

_____
(Signature)

NAME
President & CEO

REFERENCES

Anonymous. Society for Nonprofit Organizations. "Keys to a Successful Merger." *Nonprofit World.*, May/June 1992.

Austin, Gordon. 1997. "Are Chamber Mergers the Wave of the Future?" [Electronic Version] Organization: *Western Association of Chamber Executives.* Source: *Chamber Insider, Volume 29, Number 4.* City: *Sacramento, CA.* Date: *May 1997.*

Bliss, William. 2001. "Successful Integration of Merged Organizations." Bliss & Associates Inc. 2001.

Bontempo, Stacia. 2001. *Executive IdeaLink.* "Association Mergers: Special Concerns and Possible Alternatives." Chamber Executive. American Chamber of Commerce Executives. Alexandria, VA.

Elazar, Daniel. 1999. *Tocqueville and the Cultural Basis of American Democracy.* (Symposium: Tocqueville and Democracy in America) (French philosopher Alexis de Tocqueville) PS: Political Science & Politics. Issue: June 1999.

Ferronato, Sherry. 1999. "Nonprofit Mergers: Perils and Possibilities." Front & Centre, Vol. 6, No. 1.:p.1, 8-9. Canadian Centre for Philanthropy.

Fitzpatrick, Joyce. 2001. "The Board's Role in Public Relations and Communications." BoardSource.

Gardner, Natalie. June 1, 2000. "Second Harvest Merger Sets Stage for Deals." *The NonProfit Times.*

Gowdy, Heather; Kohm, Amelia; and La Piana, David, 2000. *Strategic Restructuring. Findings from a Study of Integrations and Alliances Among Nonprofit Social Service and Cultural Organizations in the United States.* Chapin Hall Center for Children.

Kramer, Donald. 2001. "Mergers and Acquisitions Can Take Many Forms." *Nonprofit Issues*, Vol. XI, No. 1, January 2001.

La Piana, David. 1994. *Nonprofit Mergers. The Board's Responsibility to Consider the Unthinkable.* BoardSource.

— 1998. *Beyond Collaboration. Strategic Restructuring of Nonprofit Organizations.* National Center for Nonprofit Boards and The James Irvine Foundation. http://www.irvine.org/frameset3.htm

— 2001a. *Resources and References. Tips.* Strategic Solutions. A Project of La Piana Associates. *Due Diligence.*

— 2001b. *Resources and References. Tips. Selecting an Executive Director Can Make Everyone Feel Like No One's In Charge.* La Piana and Associates.

— 2001c. Strategic Solutions. Tips. *Employee Relations During Strategic Restructuring.*

— 2001d. Resources and References. Tips. Funding a Strategic Restructuring Process.

— 2001e. Resources and References. Case Studies. Merger Implementation: Interview with Jan Masaoka.

— 2001f. Resources and References. Tips. Tasks of a Leadership Group during a Transition.

Leming. John. 1999. "Gaining Strength from Unity, an Argument for Mergers." *Eastern Pennsylvania Business Journal*. ACCE.

McCormick, Dan. 2001. *Nonprofit Mergers, The Power of Successful Partnerships*. Aspen Publishers, Inc.

McLaughlin, Carolyn. 1996. Mergers & Consolidations. Adress NPCC's Fall 1996 Member Reception. Copyright 1998, Nonprofit Coordinating Committee of New York.

McLaughlin, Thomas. 1996. *Seven Steps of a Successful Nonprofit Merger*. BoardSource.

Salamon, Lester. 1992. *America's Nonprofit Sector. A Primer*. The Foundation Center.

INDEX